LIVING
MORE WITH LESS

Study/Action Guide

Study/Action Guide

LIVING
MORE WITH LESS

Delores Histand Friesen

HERALD PRESS
Scottdale, Pennsylvania
Kitchener, Ontario

To those
Who dare to live
Obediently and joyfully,
Thereby freeing others
To give and receive.

"Where there is no Vision,
the People Perish."

Delores Histand Friesen

Contents

Author's Preface

Journal Entry, August 11, 1980

Lord, give me your Holy Spirit, your people in a new and fresh way, that what is done might enhance the usefulness of Doris's book. Let the study guide be such that we might account for one another, that we might support one another, that we might become one with each other—that your kingdom might come, your will be done on earth. . . .

I envision this study guide as a spur to action, a way to feel with each other, a help to decision-making, a bridge to deeper involvement in each other's lives.

Journal Entry, November 10, 1980

God, you know how easy it is for other things to crowd writing out. As I begin this morning to lay the study guide out in its final form, guide my mind and hands and heart. Let it bring out the best wine in Doris's book; let it be celebrative, enjoyable, life-changing for me and for those who read and use it.

* * *

I have written this study/action guide from the perspective of a teacher. For me, education is creating unrest, sharing visions of the possible, lending support so students can risk. Information, ideas, and right thinking are necessary; but right acting is our goal. Educational models for change require involvement, active learning, emotion, drama. In your preparation for leading study or small-group sessions, remember people are physical, social, emotional, and spiritual beings.

You will gain nothing if your sessions are grim, fact-laden, guilt-producing discussions.

This is an active study. Think serendipity. Think in terms of actions, signs of the kingdom, visibility, NOT discussion, talk, ideas. Lend hope and courage in generous measure. Work with the possible. Do things together. Give assignments of specific actions, not just pages to read. Take time for reporting on results—and frustrations. Care for one another. Keep a journal of your thoughts, insights, and feelings as you go through this course.

Living More with Less is a book which asks for change. The goal of this study guide is to integrate study and life. The study guide contains projects, questions, and resources for each of the 15 chapters in *Living More with Less,* plus an overview and a wrap-up of the entire book and a Leaders' Resource Section. Many practical suggestions are given. Hopefully, you will also create your own—ones that fit your group, your community, your family situation.

Many of the ideas and projects in the guide represent the thoughts and experiences of others. I especially appreciate those who took time to write letters expressing their support and sharing their ideas. Special thanks go to my family, Marilyn Schweitzer, Joetta Handrich, Paul Longacre, Marian Schwabbauer, Laurence Martin, and the Remnant Sunday School class at First Mennonite Church in Iowa City for their help in the writing and editing process.

Much of the study guide material can be used in intergenerational groupings and family settings. At one retreat, for example, the children created artwork, original songs, and a nature collage. These were shared with the adults and lent creativity and humor to the weekend that was much appreciated. Thus whole families were involved and the children were equally aware and thinking with the adults of how we might live more with less.

The study/action guide is designed for group interaction and personal reflection, study and action. Many of the activities and questions lend themselves well to personal inventory and action. Others will be better suited to group discussion, interchange, and counsel.

In the Leader's Resource Section, I have decided particularly to emphasize additional study guides and manuals for groups. For a more complete listing of books and audiovisual resources, I suggest that you write for the annotated bibliography prepared by Mennonite Central Committee.* In locating resources, don't forget to utilize your local libraries. If they do not have such materials available, your requests may help them to acquire these publications. You may also wish to donate resources to your church or community library.

No study guide or bibliography can be exhaustive. As we become a global village facing economic and political changes, much newly printed material will be made available. I suggest that you subscribe to at least one of the organizations or periodicals listed, so you can keep abreast of new developments, concerns, and resources. You may be able to have individual members of your group each choose one such subscription, so that together you have a wider variety of exposure.

Many of the resources are those that add the "more," and help to enhance life, rather than those which work primarily with the themes of justice, hunger, and cutting back. This does not reflect a lack of commitment to simplifying life; it grows out of my compassion for those who feel threatened by the increasing interdependence of our global village. I wish for all who read and study this book, a kind of holy joy that frees you to love and live as Jesus did—extravagantly, purposefully, obediently.

Delores Histand Friesen
Iowa City, Iowa

---

*Resources on World Hunger and Responsible Living, MCC Food and Hunger Concerns Office, 21 South 12th Street, Akron, Pa. 17501.

Settings for Using This Study/Action Guide

Because *Living More with Less* has such a varied content, it is adaptable to many types of groups and situations. Perhaps you will want to work with some combination of the following:

1. Ecumenical Settings of Study and Worship. *Living More with Less* provides very good content for such settings. It would be especially valuable to work in an ecumenical setting when one of your goals is community awareness and change.

2. Total Congregational Involvement. The worship/celebration/motivational aspects of the study could be used here. For example, a congregation could plan five Sunday morning worship services around the five life standards. These could be supplemented by small-group meetings, Sunday school class sessions, or family clustering activities.

3. Neighborhood Groups. These could include persons who are interested in the topic for other than religious reasons—humanists, social activists, local food co-ops, Cable TV, parent/teacher associations.

4. Lenten Studies for Congregation or Home Groups. The five life standards could be used for the five weeks of Lent or a different segment of the book could be used each year. Families could choose one of the Part 2 areas for their Lenten discipline each year.

5. Elective Education Hour. Some groups who use the book find enough material for from six to twelve months of study. Note bibliography listings of additional study guides. These could be used in church school, adult education classes, or public school classes, such as home economics.

6. Small Support or Accountability Groups. These could include

intentional communities, Bible study groups, a nearby neighbor family who shares your vision, your immediate family, roommates, prayer partners.

7. Family Cluster or Intergenerational Programs. Many possibilities are given which could be used in groups made up of both children and adults.

8. Workshops, Retreats, Seminars. Here the focus would need to be narrowed. You may wish to use the workshop outlines noted in the Leader's Resource Section.

9. Community Awareness. Bazaars and *Living More with Less* fairs could be planned for the community.

10. Television and Radio Talk Show Presentations.

General Overview of "Living More with Less"

In the author's foreword we are reminded that there is no fast, easy way to simple living. It can be joyful, rich, and creative, but it isn't simple. Doris Longacre, the author, reminds us that our lives are to be a perpetual response to the living God, an answer to the call to obedience.

She acknowledges that "more-with-less" standards don't come naturally in North America, but she says they can become second nature for Christians. She suggests that our way of life can be characterized by timeless values and commitments, permanent and firm, but not rigid.

Part 1 is the heart of the book. This material
—Is theological.
—Presents the framework for the rest of the book.
—Is intended to become an integral part of life.
—Is a checkup method, a plumb line against which choices and decisions can be weighed.
—Gives reasons *why* we do what we do in the ten areas in Part 2.
—Can provide themes for total congregation or community participation.

Part 2 has ten chapters. These chapters
—Are coded to demonstrate the five life standards in Part 1.
—Are introduced by excellent summary statements and principles. Make sure your group knows what the principles are. Add to the ones given, react to them. Do you have other principles by

which you make decisions in this area? In chapters 1 and 3, no principles are given. Write and create your own principles for these chapters.

—Often repeat the themes of Part 1.

—Have suggestions for further study. These resources are highly recommended, though they are not usually repeated in the study guide.

The introduction, journal entries, and foreword contain many statements that clarify the perspective, intent, and goals of the author.

If your group is not acquainted with the *More-with-Less Cookbook,* bring a copy to your first meeting. Doris introduces her second book by referring to the first:

"More with less means that by using less we actually gain more for ourselves. The opening page of the *More-with-Less Cookbook* reads, 'Put dismal thoughts aside ... because this book is not about cutting back. This book is about living joyfully, richly, and creatively.' *Living More with Less* is built on the same philosophy" (page 16). "This is a book about beauty, healing, and hope, a book about getting more, not less" (page 15).

Ron Sider says the book is an excellent combination of theory and practice, with good concrete, practical, workable models. But he makes it clear that it is not a "How To" book. Instead, he describes *Living More with Less* as:

—Testimony, pilgrimage.

—An invitation to a treasure hunt.

—A joyful exploration of the next steps toward simplicity.

—A way to find out where you are.

—A path carefully charted and joyfully trod.

—A gift to the church, the poor, and the Lord we serve.

Additional Material

1. *Symbols.* These are on page 21, on the spine of the book, and sprinkled liberally throughout. They are intended to become part of the everyday fabric of life. They can serve as guides and standards for decision making—a yardstick for how far we have come, how far we need to go.

Ji	Do Justice
L	Learn from the World Community
P	Nurture People
	Cherish the Natural Order
C	
ƒ	Nonconform Freely

2. *Boldface type items.* These denote shorter contributions, pro-verbial sayings, quotations. Many of these could be read aloud or printed on newsprint or chalkboards for visual and aural impact.

3. *Charts, pages 166-171.* Charts need to be highlighted, studied, discussed. Be alert to other similar information in your local news-papers and magazines to update and enlarge this resource.

4. *Photographs, pages 62-69.* Take time to look and respond by in-dividual journaling or two by two sharing activity. Contrast these photographs with those in *Better Homes and Gardens.* Other resources of this nature which you may want to use are *My Friends Live in Many Places* by Dorka Raynor, *Family of Man, Christian Art in Asia,* and *Christ in the Art of Africa.* This is part of a filmstrip series; available from 475 Riverside Drive, New York, N.Y.

5. *Index.* The index provides a good beginning point for several topics not given a separate chapter in the book. Conservation, for example, according to the index, is referred to in many different chapters. You could choose to build an activity or study around the entries given there. Contributors' names are not listed in the index. Names in the index refer to quotations, or footnoted material only.

6. *Biblical index.* The biblical index provides a list of quoted passages. These might be used for Bible study, devotional material, or sermon texts.

7. *Additional poetry and photographs.* Many readers miss these un-

less they are lifted out, mentioned, read aloud, savored, responded to.

8. *Blank pages.* These are at the end of the book and could be used for notes, journaling activities.

General Suggestions on How to Study Living More with Less

A thorough study of this book could take a lifetime.

You will need to be selective.

The goal of your study is not to understand and remember everything in the book.

The goal is to help people begin to make changes, to sense, feel, experience the freedom, the joy, the creativity, the more in living with less.

Help class members develop networks of caring support for the life standards they have chosen. Encourage open, free sharing. See yourself as a convener and stimulator rather than as a teacher or fact giver.

Strive to keep your group work a happy, encouraging, joyful experience. Think more in terms of consciousness raising, awareness building, than discussion and study.

The book does have an emotive quality that is appreciated in varying degrees. Some may find the quotations, poetry, and journal entries too intense. You will need to be sensitive to this as a leader, and may need to include some humor to release the tension.

But do not be afraid to let the book speak. Such writing motivates us to change. Don't be afraid to be controversial. It is in controversy that people begin to learn that something new is being said.

Plan activities. Do some in the study period itself. Have others as group and individual disciplines during the week. Put things into practice. This is far more valuable than just reading and studying the book.

Create your own *Living More with Less* book within the group. Encourage individuals to supplement the entries appearing in the ten chapters, then compile, edit, and distribute these to the group at the conclusion of the sessions.

You may wish to adapt your study to seasonal times of the year. Celebration is a good unit to do between Thanksgiving and Christmas, recreation and travel are good for summer months, and heating and new forms of energy conservation are of particular interest in winter.

Don't try to do too much. Some people may find the book too intense and feel overwhelmed. As a leader, begin by helping your group see what they are already doing in each area you will study. For example, have persons write the ten topics in Part 2 at the top of their paper. Under each one, have them list things they are already doing in these areas that illustrate standards of living more with less.

It may work best to do an overview of the book and work with the five life standards; then choose only one or two of the chapters in Part 2 to illustrate Part 1. The remaining chapters in Part 2 may be used for a repeated emphasis on living more with less the following year.

Another approach that seems to work well is to group the chapters in Part 2 under the standards in Part 1. For example, one study block could be: Nurture People from Part 1 and Celebrations, Recreation, Eating Together, and Strengthening Each Other from Part 2. Another block could be: Do Justice from Part 1 and the chapter on Money from Part 2. Cherish the Natural Order from Part 1 and Homes, Homekeeping, and Meetinghouses from Part 2.

If you are using the book as a family group, I suggest studying a portion of the book each year during Lent. Or choose a single area from Part 2 for emphasis each year. It takes time for concerns to develop and bear fruit. The following year concentrate on the issues in another chapter.

Make use of art in at least one session. This could be a creative expression from participants, a music or interpretive dance experience, or paintings from your local library. Some of my favorite paintings on a *Living More with Less* theme are: "The Gleaners" by Millet, "The Wedding" by Bosch, "Flight into Egypt" by Hitchcock, "Song of the Lark" by Breton.

The books mentioned can be ordered from the Christian bookstore nearest you or from Provident Bookstore, Box 7047, Lancaster, Pa. 17604. Most of the audiovisuals and other printed materials are available from Mennonite Central Committee, 21 South 12th Street, Akron, Pa. 17501, or Mennonite Central Committee (Canada), 201-1483 Pembina Highway, Winnipeg, Man. R3T 2C8.

LIVING
MORE WITH LESS

Study/Action Guide

Session 1

Getting Started

Goals
1. To become acquainted with the organization and the philosophy of the book.
2. To discover the concerns, interests, and experiences of your particular group.
3. To make the author's aim your own—let your group, your family, your household sing with God's message, God's glory, God's beauty!
4. To show that simple living is a deeply rooted biblical directive and not merely a fad or an approaching imperative in light of diminishing resources.
5. To develop an appreciation for the fact that happiness, freedom, contentment, and well-being are at the heart of biblical guidelines for living simply.

Study
1. What do you hope to gain from this study?
2. How can we strengthen and support one another?
3. On a scale of one to ten, rank yourself and your parents. Where are you now in living more with less? Where were/are your parents? How long have you been on the way to simplifying your life?

Action
1. On a chart or blackboard list the five standards outlined in Part 1 of *Living More with Less*. Add Bible references supporting each and invite participants to respond with more.

2. Encourage persons to share freely of their own experiences and ideas on the book's theme. We share stories to strengthen each other, not to say this is how everyone should do it. The entries in the book are not meant to imply that this book has the final answer to more-with-less living.

3. If persons in your group were personally acquainted with the author, they may wish to share something from their friendship.

4. Talk together in groups of three or four about expectations for your study. Write these on newsprint or a chalkboard. Be sure they are met throughout the study. Preview the projects suggested on pages 92 and 93.

5. Look at the table of contents. In Part 2, choose two or three areas in which you feel you have something to share. Choose two or three where you feel you need to learn and grow.

6. Make a large size version of the five symbols, using clay, felt, burlap, or felt-tip markers and newsprint. Put your visual in a conspicuous place. Encourage participants to do the same in their homes. Perhaps your group will have additional symbols to suggest that help make the five life standards memorable. For example, one person suggested representing nonconform freely by a backwards F.

7. To highlight the boldface-type items, read aloud the Japanese poet's entry on page 20, or use the first entry on page 14 as a choric. Divide into two groups and read aloud, alternating lines, then join together in the final prayer.

8. Look at the charts on pages 166-170. Note, for example, that the United States consumes twice as much energy per capita as the United Kingdom and Germany; four times as much as Japan! (p. 166). As income goes up, spending for housing and miscellaneous triples. Personal taxes become six times greater! (p. 169). Frostless refrigerators consume twice as much energy as standard models (p. 168).

9. Use the motivation quiz in the Leader's Resource Section, page 93, to arouse interest.

10. Be sure participants understand the coding system between the symbols of Part 1 and entries in Part 2.

Resources

Introduction, Journal Entries, Foreword, pages 1-20 of *Living More with Less.*

More-with-Less Cookbook, Herald Press, 1976.

Living More with Less—A Choric. Plan to use this choric sometime during the study either in the class session or in a church service. It is in the Leader's Resource Section, page 95.

Living More with Less, MCC Cassette, 14 minutes, available 21 South 12th Street, Akron, Pa. 17501, or MCC 201-1483 Pembina Highway, Winnipeg, Man. R3T 2C8.

How to Conduct a More-with-Less Workshop, MCC Cassette, 19 minutes. This cassette is an accompaniment to the new book of the same name by Doris Janzen Longacre. Side one introduces listeners to the book, or can serve as an additional resource for a speaker or workshop leader speaking on more-with-less themes. Side two was recorded by Doris Longacre to assist persons leading workshops on the *More-with-Less Cookbook.* Her instructions are applicable to the new book as well. Addresses above.

Session 2

Do Justice

Goals

1. To develop attentiveness to the needs of others so we can live by both reason and compassion.
2. To observe the connections in a global community.
3. To examine those attitudes which foster justice for all.
4. To realize that justice will come primarily through economic and political change.
5. To become acquainted with some of the strategies that are being proposed to overcome poverty and hunger.
6. To become familiar with some basic Scripture passages on hunger.
7. To connect the message of Scripture with the actual life situation of today's world.

Study

1. If recycling, conserving, sharing are the firstfruits of the harvest of justice, what will, what does, the full harvest look like?

2. Is some practical political or economic change needed in our local community?

3. How do salvation and justice relate to each other? Consider Luke 3:7-14.

4. What is one way I personally do justice? If this is hard for your group to answer, discuss why we shy away from involvement in this area.

5. Do newspaper articles and TV increase or decrease our sensitivity to world problems? How can you make others more sensitive to areas of human need?

Action

1. If you did not use it in Session 1, take the quiz in the Leader's Resource Section on page 93 or make up your own awareness-raising questions.

2. List ways you are presently involved in the political/economic sphere. Contact agencies in your community that are helping people to achieve their basic human rights.

3. Keep track of your mail for one week. Lay it in three stacks: How much nurtures people, promotes consumption (ads, coupons), encourages you to do justice? Which stack is the largest? Smallest? How might you change this imbalance? Have several persons display their stacks of mail.

4. Bring sample magazines and mailings that promote justice, for example, *The Other Side, Sojourners, Fellowship of Reconciliation, Daughters of Sarah, Bread for the World, Amnesty International.*

5. Have volunteers write to the organizations listed on page 29 of Doris's book and in the resources section of this session for literature or subscriptions.

6. Decide to tax yourself voluntarily each time you purchase an item that comes from the Third World, i.e., bananas, sugar, coffee, tea, tuna, pineapple. See page 84 in *Living More with Less,* and page 101 in the Leader's Resource Section (#7).

7. Role play the opening incident of the envelopes. One class began its discussion, and was startled when one member walked in late and addressed his wife, "The reverberation of this wasteful act will be felt around the world." She had been quietly discarding envelopes and paper, but few class members had noticed.

8. Provide paper, addresses of Congress persons or Parliament members, and a list of topics about which persons could write to their representatives.

9. Find out how justice issues such as hunger are taught in the schools in your community. Examine textbooks and classroom materials. Develop or suggest alternate curricula and special events that present another view.

10. Choose to become thoroughly familiar with the forces causing hunger and injustice in one country.

11. Read the story of Joseph in Genesis 41:46-57. Discuss the implications of this story in connection with the call for an international grain reserve system. See page 28 in *Living More with Less.*

12. Visit the supermarket and determine what foods, including

fresh fruits and vegetables, are imported by the U.S. or Canada.

13. Imagine that you have to talk to someone who does not know about God. Describe the God who reveals himself in the Bible. How does he relate to people? About whom does he care? What does he think is important?

14. Divide the group into two teams to debate this opinion: "Ordinary citizens have no power in influencing public policy. The big companies control the government."

15. Explore the idea that citizenship is a gift of God. It is another gift that we can use on behalf of the hungry and dispossessed poor of the world.

16. Make collages of pictures and/or music depicting the biblical mandate to seek justice.

17. Doing justice requires that we take a stand on economic and political issues. Solutions for Third World needs will come primarily through economic and political change. Have your group respond to these conclusions.

18. Find out who is hungry in your neighborhood, and why. Help dispel myths about hunger in conversations with friends and acquaintances. Share a meal with a lonely or needy person in your church or neighborhood. Help deliver Meals on Wheels.

19. Respond to Rudolf Dyck's critique, "Doris's concept of justice at the international level needs expansion. The author implies that the world's poor are so because we are rich. This is too simple. Poverty has many causes, one of which is the lack of credit institutions for capital formation. Another is the problem of over-breeding, particularly in relation to developed resources. Callous and corrupt governments in the third world is a further cause of poverty. Seldom is poverty, in my opinion, caused by exploitation by the multinational corporations." (From a review of *Living More with Less,* by Rudolf Dyck, in *Festival Quarterly,* p. 3, May, June, July, 1980.)

20. Adopt an Amnesty International prisoner. Help work for the release of men and women detained for their beliefs, color, sex, ethnic origin, language, or religion, who have neither used nor advocated violence. Pray for the innocent victims of torture and other acts of oppression.

21. Reflect on a time in your life when a person who had power over you treated you badly and affected you adversely. Reflect on a time when a person who had power over you has helped you in some way or treated you with respect and kindness.

22. Plan a hunger awareness dinner. See Van Beilen's book for ideas.

Resources

Simulation Game:

"Starpower," Simile 11, P.O. Box 1023, La Jolla, Calif. 92037, $3.00. Simulation game that deals with the unequal distribution of wealth and power. Initially, participants have a chance to progress from one level of society to another through trading. However, society soon becomes fixed and the group with the most wealth makes the rules of the game.

Hunger Awareness Dinners, by Aileen van Beilen, Herald Press, contains directions for several adaptations of meals and refreshments to help persons realize how uneven food distribution feels.

Hunger Activities for Teens and *Hunger Activities for Children,* Brethren House Ministries, 1979, 6301-56th Avenue, N., St. Petersburg, Fla. 33709.

Audiovisuals

Sights and Sounds of Hunger, audiovisual kit, available from Mennonite Central Committee. Includes 4 filmstrips, 12 frames each: "How Some People Live," "Where Is the Water?" "Where Is the Food?" "World Relief Helps"; 5 cassette tapes, 16 teaching pictures, and *Teacher's Guidebook.* Supplements the book *Hunger Activities for Children.*

The Hangman. Twelve-minute animated color film which asks whether any person has the choice of not speaking out against injustice done to others. It rents for $15.00 and can be ordered from United Methodist Film Service, 1525 McGavock St., Nashville, Tenn. 37203.

"A World Hungry," Teleketics. Five-part filmstrip series on hunger, its causes and solutions, as well as Christian responses to the hungry. Accompanied by a chart and other good teaching material. Available from MCC, and many other denominational A-V centers.

"Tilt," American Friends Service Committee. A 19-minute animated film about the way in which the world's wealth is shared. $5.00 rental fee.

Bread for the World Filmstrips may be borrowed for the cost of postage. Available from MCC.

Music
"Sermon on the Mount," 97, *Sing and Rejoice!* (Herald Press, 1979)
"Obey My Voice," 69, *Sing and Rejoice!*
"What Will I Do?" 134, *Sing and Rejoice!*

Organizations
Institute for Food and Development Policy
2588 Mission Street
San Francisco, Calif. 94110

Amnesty International, USA
2112 Broadway
New York, N.Y. 10023

IMPACT
110 Maryland Ave., N.E.
Washington, D.C. 20002

Bread for the World
207 East 16th St.
New York, N.Y. 10003

MCC Peace Section
100 Maryland Ave., N.E.
Washington, D.C. 20002

For obtaining material for workshop resources, see the item on page 110.

Bible Study or Sermon Ideas
Justice is a central concern in the Scriptures. In creation, Yahweh calls his people to be copartners with him in this work. Later he saves the oppressed who in turn are to be concerned for those who are unjustly treated. The prophets proclaim a message of justice for the poor. Jesus is the fulfillment of God's concern for his people.

Some Topics and Scriptures to Get You Started
Justice: The mission of the servant of the Lord—Isaiah 42:1-9
Biblical Concepts of Shalom and Jubilee—Deuteronomy 14:28-15:11;
    Psalm 112, Psalm 15, Proverbs 14:21
Justice: The Foundation of Peace—Isaiah 3:13-15, Psalm 112
Justice and Worship Are Bound Together—Matthew 5:23 f.; Isaiah
    1:11-17; 58:6-11; Deuteronomy 24:14, 15, 22, Prov. 19:17, 21:13
God's Passion for Justice—Amos 5:21-24; Micah 6:9; Deuteronomy
    10:17-20; Psalm 82
Yahweh: Defender of the Oppressed—Exodus 22:21-22; Deuteronomy
    14:28, 29; 10:18; Psalm 103:6; 146:7-9

Share Your Bread with the Hungry—Isaiah 58:6-9, 8-10; Deuteronomy
    19:9-10; Amos 2:7; 5:11, 21-24
New Testament Teachings on Justice—Luke 3:11; 4:18-19; 12:48; Mat-
    thew 4:2; 5:13-16; 13:1-52; 15:29-39; 25:31-46; James 2:14-17;
    Romans 12:1-21; 1 John 3:16-4:21, Acts 2:42-47
Create a modern version of a New Testament story that works with justice and hunger issues, i.e. Lazarus and the rich man, Zacchaeus, the
rich young ruler. Dramatize feelings, the internal process of decision
making and community reaction to what happened.

Session 3

Learn from the World Community

Goals
1. To create an awareness of the contribution the world community can make to North America.
2. To help participants gain an appreciation for other cultures.
3. To examine the concept of global community.
4. To enjoy learning from cross-cultural perspectives.

Study
1. Global interdependence is increasing. What we do *does* make a difference. The way we live affects the world community. Do you agree with Doris that we are first of all citizens of the earth and secondly citizens of a country?

2. Before you can appreciate and learn from another culture, you need to appreciate and understand the strengths and weaknesses of your own culture. What do you appreciate about your country and culture? What would you like to change?

3. How do the Europeans and Japanese manage a high standard of living with less than half the energy consumption per person in North America? See chart on page 166.

4. When is travel to another country justified? What have you learned from such cross-cultural travel?

5. Why is it so hard for Americans to accept the role of learner? Do you think North Americans have a superiority complex?

6. What do you think about the author's statement about our *over*development or *mal*development being as much of a concern as the *under*development of poor nations? How are we overdeveloped?

Action

1. Rank the seven projects listed in the text, pages 31-34. Which ones do you feel are most important? Which ones are you already doing?

2. Have someone who has lived in another country share what they have learned and incorporated into their present-day living.

3. Demonstrate cooking Chinese stir-fried vegetables followed by a tasting party.

4. Become involved with refugee families in your neighborhood or volunteer for International Host Family programs. Offer hospitality to persons from other countries. Get to know at least one new international friend each year.

5. Use the photographs and quotations, pages 61-70, for group reflection and/or a journaling activity.

6. Notice how little international news is included in our news programs and papers. What media have you found that share world happenings?

7. Have someone from another culture share that culture's way of living: celebration, recreation, and family activities.

8. Divide into small groups to discuss what participants have learned from the world community through overseas experiences, neighbors from other cultures, grandparents from another era.

Scriptures

Dramatize or discuss Jesus' encounter with the Samaritan woman, John 4:1-42, or the story of the Good Samaritan, Luke 10:29-37, from the standpoint of this chapter. How did Jesus relate to persons of another culture?

Use the responsive reading, *Body and Bread,* page 98 in the Leader's Resource Section.

Music

"In Christ There Is No East or West," 387, *The Mennonite Hymnal*

"I Bind My Heart This Tide," 353, *The Mennonite Hymnal*

"Blest Be the Tie That Binds," 385, *The Mennonite Hymnal*

"Heart with Loving Heart United," 386, *The Mennonite Hymnal*

Books

"I Lay on My Mat and Pray," edited by Fritz Pavelock, *Prayers from African Young People.*

My Friends Live in Many Places, Dorka Raynor, Albert Whitman, 1980.

Enough Is Enough, John V. Taylor, SCM Press, 1975, Augsburg, 1977. Well documented, builds world awareness and global interdependence.

Nectar in a Sieve, Kamala Markandaya, John Day, 1954. Beautiful and eloquent story of a peasant woman in India.

The Spring Wind, Gladis Depree. Reflections on what an American family learned in Hong Kong.

In Every Person Who Hopes, James and Margaret Goff, Friendship Press, New York, 1980. See especially the section entitled "Expressions of Protest and Hope" written by South Americans.

UNICEF Book of Children's Poems by William Kaufman, Stackpole Books, 1970.

Audiovisuals

"The Way of Tea" and "Two People," Maryknoll Film Libraries. Order from Maryknoll Fathers, Walsh Building, Pinesbridge Road, Maryknoll, N.Y. 10545. Free rental. Both build cross-cultural awareness.

Periodicals

The Other Side and *Christian Science Monitor* are especially helpful for learning from the World Community. (See the Leader's Resource Section, p. 109 for addresses.)

Session 4

Nurture People

Goals
1. To encourage more nurturing of ourselves and others.
2. To see people as more important than material things.

Study
1. Is it true that when every possible need is satisfied before we even have a chance to perceive and respond to it, creativity and resourcefulness can't flourish? Are our children short-changed?

2. Doris lists some of the drawbacks of a technological society as follows:

—Atrophy of our ability to respond resourcefully to the environment
—Damaging to the human spirit
—Things offered as imitation love
—Dependence on machines is bad for the human body
—Society is overstimulated

What are the advantages of a technological society?

3. How do persons become strong inside? See Motlalpula Chabaku's comment on page 42.

4. How do you maintain strong relationships with family and friends who live far away?

5. What is nurturing? See pages 37-42.

Action
1. Write a letter to someone who has influenced your life, someone who has nurtured you—other than your parents, perhaps.

2. Do a journaling exercise. Make a list of the ways you nurture your body, your mind, your spirit.

3. If you are a parent, list ways you consciously try to nurture your child, emotionally, spiritually, and physically.

4. Play a cooperative game together, where everyone wins.

5. Spend time this week being more genuinely affectionate. This may mean more touching and hugging. See the resources list below if you need touching exercises.

6. Invite a friend to lunch, or call or write a faraway friend.

7. Share ways you depend on God, on your family and friends.

8. Take a health habit inventory, using the list on page 41.

9. As a group, discuss the concept of throwing away human resources. Our society has largely succeeded in throwing away people over sixty. How can we make our older adults feel like a valuable part of society? Have a party for older adults or volunteer to do some work around their homes. Show them you haven't thrown them away.

Scriptures
These could be used for study, worship, or drama presentations.

Ruth 1	Esther 2:5-7
Leviticus 19:17, 18	Exodus 2:1-10—would lend itself to a character sketch or simple drama of the ways Moses was nurtured by his two "mothers"
Matthew 5:43-48	
Luke 15	Matthew 19:13-15; Luke 18:15-17 Jesus and the children
Matthew 18:1-35	

Books
Peoplemaking, Virginia Satir, Science and Behavior Book, 1972.
T.S.K.H. (Tickle, Snug, Kiss, Hug), Elizabeth May, Paulist Press, 1977.
Be Your Own Best Friend, Newman and Berkowitz, Ballatine, 1975.
The Friendship Factor, McGinnis, Augsburg, 1979.
The Heart of Friendship, James and Savary, Harper, 1978.
Big Sister and Little Sister, Charlotte Zolotow, Harper, 1966.
   Excellent presentation of idea that even "strong" people need nurture.
The Way Mothers Are, Miriam Schlein, Whitman, 1967.

Images, Women in Transition, compiled by Janice Grana, The Upper Room, 1976.

Cooperative Games and Sports, Terry Orlick, Pantheon, 1978.

Raising Your Child by Love Not by Force, Sidney D. Craig, Westminster. Suggests creating a "Love Bank" for each child.

Anytime Book for Busy Families, Zinciewicz, Upper Room.

Honey for a Child's Heart, Gladys Hunt, Zondervan.

Summer of the Great-Grandmother, Madeline L. Engle, Seabury, 1979.

From Married to Merried, L. Richard Lessor, Argus Communications, 1972, creative ways to enhance relationships and nurture one another.

Audiovisuals

The Chairy Tale. Silent film, humorous, brief. Teaches mutual respect, honor, care. Rental $3.00 from Box 347, Newton, Kans. 67114, or your public library.

Annie and the Old One. Beautiful North American Indian film available at most public libraries. Works with life and death issues, acceptance of what is to be, value of work, integrity of aging. Based on children's book by same title.

The Velveteen Rabbit, by Margery Williams, filmstrip, Alba House Communications, 1977, color, 10 minutes, all ages. This set of two filmstrips is an illustration of the book of the same name by Margery Williams. The message of the Velveteen Rabbit is universally and timelessly true, "You aren't real until somebody really loves you."

Games

"Ungame." A noncompetitive board game which focuses on communication. It nurtures people by helping players better understand themselves and each other. There are additional sets of cards for married couples, students, families. Spanish cards are also available.

Music

"Love, Love, Love," 68, *Sing and Rejoice!*

"Agape Meal Song," 2, *Sing and Rejoice!*

Session 5

Cherish the Natural Order

Goals

1. To understand that the gifts of God are held in trust and are to be used for the upbuilding of the community.
2. To prompt actions that respect and honor natural resources.
3. To set conservation and recycling concerns in a context of the biblical understanding of creation.

Study

1. Are we pitted in a battle against nature? Is this what God intended when he created man and told him to have dominion over the earth and everything in it?

2. Is the world's wealth a common possession of all humanity? What about the resources in the world's oceans? Do those belong only to the countries which border the oceans?

3. How can we consciously choose to fit the way we live to the environment, rather than trying to reshape the environment to our wants?

4. What do we do when environmental protection costs us more than the old system of using up, throwing away, and destroying?

Action

1. Write a rebuttal to the ad on page 44; debate the ad's content. Find similar ads in magazines.

2. If your state does not have a bottle and can recycling law, investigate getting one. Let persons who have lived in states, with and without recycling laws, report on the differences in litter and roadside cleanliness.

3. Share recycling stories and recycled items.

4. Take a field trip to see solar energy projects in your area.

5. Do a water count. All day long, make a note every time you use some water. How many gallons do you think you use? Every flush of a toilet takes eight gallons of water.

6. Try the "No bag, please" experiment. Next time you go shopping, take a big bag along. When you buy something, say, "I don't need a bag, thanks." Note how the clerk acts. You will soon find out how hard it is for people to get used to saving paper (from *Save the Earth*, page 26).

7. This chapter would lend itself to an outdoor experience. Consider a weekend retreat, or day-long picnic. Ask participants to bring in signs or symbols from nature that illustrate the life standards.

8. Have the group debate this opinion: "People living in the world today have an obligation to use fewer resources from the earth so that future generations will have access to these resources."

9. Bring a bag of "trash" (cereal boxes, aluminum containers, plastic bags) to prompt discussion on recycling and reusing.

10. Visit a recycling center near you. Discover how our old bottles, cans, and newspapers are made reusable. Ask your church council if you can supply a "drop-off" spot at your church. Have church members bring their paper, bottles, and cans to this spot for recycling. Be sure to print instructions in the church bulletin about how to prepare bottles and cans for recycling. Many centers refuse cans and bottles that are not clean.

11. Create a worship service focusing on why Christians should be concerned about hunger and the wasting of resources. Invite people to bring garbage and throw it in a big trash barrel as they enter. Focus on what we throw away, how much we waste, and also how much "garbage" we have within our personal lives.

12. Make a display of nature scenes and postcards for your classroom.

13. Put a brick in the tank of your toilet. This still leaves enough water to flush most toilets but saves the amount of water displaced by the brick—every time the toilet is flushed!

Resources

Use the creation accounts in Genesis 1 and 2 to discover principles for our relationship to the earth. See pages 45 and 46 in *Living More with Less* as a beginning.

Look at the Old Testament theology of land. See Leviticus 25; Isaiah
5:8; Amos 5:24; Psalm 24:1. For a description of pollution and its
effects, see Isaiah 24:4-6, 11.

Use the song "Let's Take Care of God's Good Earth" on page 99 and
the Ecology Checkup on page 100 in the Leader's Resource Section.

Books and Magazines

Energy Future, Stobaugh and Yergin, Ballatine 1979.

Why the Sky Is Far Away. African folktale that encourages using only
what you need. Retold by Mary-Joan Gerson, Harcourt Brace
Jovanovich, 1974.

Save the Earth by Betty Miles, Knopf, 1974. A first-class ecology book
for young people; includes a How to Do It section, projects, ex-
periments.

The Lorax, Random House, 1971. Dr. Seuss's classic on pollution,
consumption, extinction, and the mechanized society. Great for
both adults and children.

The Oxcart Man, Donald Hall, Viking, 1979.

The Mushroom Center Disaster, N. M. Bodecker, Atheneum, 1974.
Very ingenious, creative ideas for recycling.

Island of the Blue Dolphins, Scott O'Dell, Dell paperback, 1978.

The Compost Heap, Harlow Rockwell, Doubleday, 1974.

National Geographic World, Arizona Highways, Ranger Rick, and other
nature magazines. Borrow from your local library.

Everyday Prayers, Madeleine L'Engle, Morehouse-Barlow, 1974.

Earthkeeping, Lored Wilkinson, Eerdmans, 1980.

Farming the Lord's Land, Charles P. Lutz, Augsburg, 1980.

Audiovisuals

Stripmining and Appalachia, produced by Appalshop, 1973, 20 minutes,
16mm film, junior high-adult. Order from MCC, 21 South 12th
Street, Akron, Pa. 17501.

Session 6

Nonconform Freely

Goals
1. To gain courage and support for change.
2. To experience the freedom and joy of nonconforming.

Study
1. Do you agree with the author that the questions "Can we pay for it?" and "Is it scientifically possible?" are conformed-to-the-world questions? How do we get our priorities in the right order?

2. The pressures to conform and consume are very real, especially for teenagers. How do you deal with, or help your children deal with, the feeling of not being in the same league with your peers? See page 56.

3. Do material things threaten our freedom? How? See page 54. How do we learn to appreciate the freedom of not being enslaved to material things? How do we teach this freedom to our children?

4. What are some examples of nonconforming from your parents' or grandparents' generation that might be useful today?

5. Discuss ways we allow ourselves to become fragmented and self-destructive by allowing external forces to control our lives. How can we guard against their influence?

> —Advertisements convince us we are not okay without their products.
> —Overstimulated with things to do, see, hear, and enjoy, we do not take time to center ourselves in a broader perspective.
> —Expecting perfection of ourselves, we concentrate on our failures rather than progress, weakness rather than strength, problems rather than what we can accomplish.

6. Competition, mobility, and personal independence are forces that undermine our ability to nonconform freely. How can we combat, defuse, and redirect these forces?

Action

1. Write down the names of persons who support, encourage, and strengthen your resolves to live more simply.

2. Make another list of persons whom you influence, support, and encourage to live more simply.

3. Organize a Television Awareness Training workshop for your community. Write to Media Action Research Center, Inc., Suite 1370, 475 Riverside Dr., New York, N.Y. 10115, or call 1-212-865-6690; or contact TAT Canada, Rev. Keith Woollard, 85 St. Clair East, Toronto, M4T 1M8, Canada.

4. When ads come on the TV or radio, do something to lessen their impact. Leave the room for snack or toilet break; talk back to the advertiser, turn the volume down.

5. Copy and post the quotations in large print on pages 53, 55, 56, on newsprint, chalkboards, or bulletin boards.

6. Play the catalog game suggested on page 217.

7. Write a letter to an advertiser whose ads you wish to call into question, or whose program you want to encourage. James Dobson says each letter counts for 4000 viewers. Television Awareness Training says every letter counts for 400 viewers. This means a group of ten letters could have quite an impact. By law all letters to radio and TV must be kept on permanent file.

8. Distribute magazines. Have persons find advertisements that entice us to use their products. List the values these advertisements represent.

9. Arrange in advance for several people to share a family experience of nonconforming freely. Explore feelings, difficulties, and rewards of the experience.

10. Think of something you "couldn't live without." Consider which of your needs it meets. This can be anything from a morning shower, to a cup of coffee, to going to church on Sunday. Try giving this up for a time and record your feelings. By upgrading your addictions to preferences, you are not controlled by your "need" for them.

11. Role play one of the following situations of nonconforming to show how attitudes can vary. Discuss the attitudes that emerge. How can negative attitudes be transformed?

—Your family of four is on a low-budget vacation, camping in a small tent. Neighboring campers have much more convenient accommodations. What attitudes surface in family discussions about the differences?

—The new Sears catalog has just arrived. Your adolescent child has browsed its pages and made a large order for new clothing. The two of you attempt to pare down the list.

—You and your spouse are driving home from a visit with friends who have just made renovations in their house. Your conversation drifts to that. What attitudes emerge?

12. Make a list of the ways Jesus nonconformed. He did lots of things considered wrong by others.

Books

The Upside-Down Kingdom, Donald B. Kraybill, Herald Press, 1978.

A Kid's Guide to TV, Joy Wilt, Word, 1977. A fun book with an impact, especially the chapter on TV advertising. Humorous, cartoon style, hard to miss the message.

Television Awareness Training, the viewer's guide for family and community edited by Ben Logan. Media Action Resource Center, Inc., 1979. Contains resources, articles, and observation guides.

Alternate Celebrations Catalog, Alternatives, Inc., 1978. Ideas for alternate ways to celebrate life, death, weddings, holidays, gift giving.

Small Is Beautiful, Economics as If People Mattered, E. S. Schumacher, Harper, 1973.

Celebration of Discipline, Richard J. Foster, Harper, 1978.

Living Together in a World Falling Apart and *Coming Together,* Dave and Neta Jackson, Bethany Fellowship, 1978.

The Hundred Dresses, Eleanor Estes, Harcourt Brace Jovanovitch, 1974.

John J. Plenty and Fiddler Dan, John Ciardi. Delightful children's humorous poetry book that shows how persons with conflicting values and lifestyles see each other. Contrasts values of hard work and squirreling it away with celebrative freedom.

Partnership, Edward Dufresne, Paulist, 1975. Especially chapter 7, "The Sign of Madness: Time and Possessions in Marriage."

Music

"Teach Me Kingdom Ways," 102, *Sing and Rejoice!*

"Fill My House unto the Fullest," 24, *Sing and Rejoice!*
"O Freedom," 89, *Sing and Rejoice!*

Scriptures and Sermon Idea

Matthew 6:19-34, 7:13-14	Romans 12:1-2
Luke 12:15	1 Peter 2:16
Matthew 5:43-48	John 8:32

The Way of Resistance: *Matthew 6:22-24, 7:13-14*
    1) Unify the spirit—Keep your eye single
    2) Answer the call—Enter the narrow gate
    3) The hard way leads to life

The supreme call is to unify one's life. From being divided among a thousand things we are asked to see all things in the light of a single loyalty.

Simplicity is nothing less than a disengagement of the heart. It is a return to one Master, with a heart set on a single purpose. Keep our eye simple—see all things, but delight in only one. Simplicity is not grinding poverty; it is not having nothing, but needing little. Living simply means restoring the connection between personal needs and the necessities of life.

Simplicity gives us deep solidarity with the poor; no competition with the rich. Simplicity gives us the freedom of compassion in a world of rivalries.

—Ideas from Dufresne, *Partnership,*
pages 115-117.

Session 7

Money

Goals

1. To redefine and limit the power of money in our lives.
2. To see that our use of money is a basic biblical issue.
3. To examine how time, convenience, and money are closely related in our decisions of daily life.

Study

1. Why is it so hard to share specific information about our money situation and decisions with our brothers and sisters in Christ? Do you give and accept counsel on how money is earned and used?

2. If money is not the only old-age security, what else is? What can we do to assure a joyous old age?

3. What are some guidelines for investing money?

4. Why/how has shopping and buying become recreation?

5. How can we unchain ourselves from the belief that time is money? Does time wound you? Or does it heal you? See pages 75, 76.

6. How do you presently limit the power of money in your life?

7. Some people set salaries or limit their income to match their necessities. If they receive money above a certain level, they use it as opportunity for self-expression. What do you think about this approach?

8. Do your purchasing decisions include such questions as where to buy? Who benefited and who got hurt in its production? Will it last? Can it be used in more than one way?

9. Why do we relate human worth to monetary value? How can we resist this societal pressure?

10. Are good money decisions mostly a matter of thrift and

frugality? Does living more with less sometimes mean paying more money? A rather important emphasis of Doris's is justice vs. cheapness, quality vs. price.

Action

1. Begin your study by role playing or discussing the incident on page 73 in *Living More With Less*.

2. Divide into groups of from 2 to 4 and share some of the following recollections or use them as a journaling exercise.

What is your happiest memory in connection with money?

What is your unhappiest memory?

What role did money have in your childhood? What attitude did your mother have toward money? What attitude did your father have? What was your attitude toward money as a child? As a teenager? As a young adult? As a parent? Did you feel poor? Or rich? Did you worry about money? Did your attitude or feelings shift at different stages in your life? (From Elizabeth O'Connor, *Letters to Scattered Pilgrims,* p. 28-30.)

3. Write down how your family's consumption patterns would be different if you lived in a neighborhood where the average income was $10,000, then $25,000, and finally in a neighborhood where the average income was $45,000.

4. If there are professional persons in your group, it may be timely to discuss how others might follow the examples given on pages 80, 81, 87, 88, 89, 96.

5. Write for information about how you can invest your savings in church or charitable institutions. In the Mennonite Church, for example, persons can invest their savings in either the Mission Board or the Publishing House. See page 91.

6. As a discipline, keep track of every penny you spend for one week or one month. Plot or graph where your money goes. Share varying percentages spent by persons in your group for essentials such as housing, food, clothing, transportation. For example, in one class, house payments varied from zero to $500 per month. This is an immediate step to more open financial sharing, and may help some become aware for the first time of where their money goes.

7. Plan yearly for a fixed level of spending for your household. Give to help those in need according to Ron Sider's graduated tithe described in *The Christian Entrepreneur* by Carl Kreider, Herald Press. See pages 148, 149.

8. This chapter, unlike most of the ones that follow, has no principles clearly outlined. Decide as a group what some principles might be for this chapter. Write them on newsprint, or add them to your book. See the entries on pages 83, 84 and page 91 for examples of principles some persons use.

9. Count the money in your pocket or purse. What is the range in your group? This may vary from under $1.00 to over $100. If you wish, talk about how much money you need to feel comfortable and secure.

10. Have people bring their checkbooks to the meeting. Spend some time marking your checkbook with the five life standard symbols. For example, the phone bill might be marked nurture people, the subscription to *The Other Side* is learning from the world community. Continue this exercise. How do the five life standards interact with your finances?

11. Evaluate your money priorities. Close your eyes. Imagine that you have received a windfall of $15,000, the only condition being that you must spend it within two weeks. Decide how you will spend it. Open your eyes and jot down your list of expenditures. Now compare notes with your partner, discussing the values which guided your decisions.

12. The money chapter is something of a microcosm of the rest of the book. It covers theology, weaves in justice and nonconformity themes, and has the most biblical material. You may need to take several sessions to do it justice or may find it good to come back to it at the end of your study of *Living More with Less*.

13. Have a barter. See how much fun it is to trade items without the use of money. See pages 92 and 93. Bring items which you wish to give away or trade. Or write down services, skills you have which you would be willing to exchange—i.e., baking homemade bread, giving piano lessons, changing oil, making simple household repairs. These could be written on a piece of paper and put in a hat, then drawn like names for Christmas exchanges.

14. Investigate your local bank's investments. See page 83. For a copy of a letter form which can be used to withdraw accounts, write to: The Committee to Oppose Bank Loans to South Africa, 305 East 46th Street, New York, N.Y. 10017.

15. Try the self-imposed excise tax on imported products from which workers do not get adequate compensation. This could include food, clothing, and manufactured items. See Suggestions for a Self-Imposed Luxury Tax, page 101, in the Leader's Resource Section.

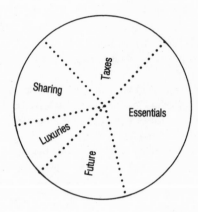

16. *Slicing a pie.* Draw on a chalkboard a circle, which is to represent a "pie" of family spending. To the right of the circle list the following items:

a. Taxes (spending I have no control over)
b. Essentials (basic foods, transportation, shelter, clothing)
c. Luxuries (entertainment, snacks, recreation, vacation, conveniences)
d. Future security (savings, insurances, social security, pension plans, stocks)
e. Sharing (personal gifts, charities, church offerings)

Pass out pencils and paper and instruct members of the group to draw their own pie and to divide it into five pieces representing the five categories indicated. The pieces should correspond in size to the percentage of income which one feels should be spent ideally for the five categories of spending. When each person has completed his or her pie, share the results. Discuss the question: Do our suggestions for slicing the pie of spending reflect the values of the simple life? Why or why not? As a take-home assignment, ask each person to review the way his or her family actually does spend its income and to draw a second pie representing those percentages.

—*A Plain People* by Thomas E. Ryan, page 28

17. Discuss John F. Kennedy's comment that we need to take care of the poor so that we can guarantee the survival of the rich.

18. If your community has a co-op, visit it. If there is not one in your community, discuss ways of beginning some kind of cooperative buying.

19. Create a toy lending library for disadvantaged children in your neighborhood.

20. Find out what items your group or your church would be willing to share on a loan or small rental basis, i.e., rototillers, slide projectors, baby furniture, carriers, car seats, sports and camping equipment. You may wish to include your loan library list in the back of your church directory. See page 92.

21. Figure out what the giving level of your congregation would be if every adult in your church tithed a median income of $8,000 per adult. Look at the giving patterns in your group. Are they affected by inflation?

22. This chapter lends itself well to writing your own testimonies. The boldface headings Doris uses will get you started. For example, how do you budget and share? How do you lend and borrow?

23. Identify with the poor. Find out what the welfare budget is for a family your size in your area. Plan to live on that for a month or several months. Decide as a family, or as a group of families how you will use the money saved.

Bible Study or Sermon Ideas

Survey what the Bible says about money. Have group members use
    their concordances to find references and stories about money.
Substantiate Wallace Fisher's comment that Jesus spoke five times as
    much about money and earthly possessions as about prayer.
Do a role play of the rich young ruler story set in modern times.
Memorize some of the following: Proverbs 30:7-9; 2 Corinthians 8:12-
    15, 9:6-12; 1 John 3:17, 18; Matthew 6:21; 1 Timothy 6:10.

Books and Pamphlets

"Property attitudes checklist," pages 130, 132, in John W. Miller, *The
    Christian Way,* Herald press, 1969.
The Christian Entrepreneur, Carl Kreider, Herald Press, 1980.
Stewards of God, Milo Kauffman, Herald Press, 1975.
Tit for Tat, Dorothy O. Van Woerkom, Greenwillow Books, 1977. A
    fanciful humorous tale of how what we do in the morning affects
    us all day, how greed interacts with human need. Contrasts a giv-
    ing person with a selfish miser. "Whatever he had he kept for

himself. And whatever he had was never enough" (page 10).

The Way of True Riches, Milo Kauffman, Herald Press, 1979.

What Mennonites Believe About Money, Mennonite Publishing House, 1980, Larry Kehler.

The Graduated Tithe, Ronald J. Sider, Pamphlet, 1978.

Letters to Scattered Pilgrims, Elizabeth O'Connor. Harper, 1979.

Be sure to note Resources listed on page 79 of *Living More with Less*.

Session 8

Clothes

Goals
1. To identify living more with less principles that apply to clothing purchase and use.
2. To learn ways to cut back investments of time, money, and concern with what we wear.
3. To consider questions of quality, quantity, style, and nonconformity in clothing.

Study
1. Is it possible for clothing adaptations to make a significant difference in the amount of energy we use to change our indoor temperature? See pages 101 and 102.

2. What ways have you found to express your personality through dress without allowing clothing to become an answer to boredom or a substitute for inner resources of self-assurance? How do you help teenagers deal with this question?

3. How do you avoid unnecessary clashes over clothing with your children? How can we accept differing tastes without hassling and creating barriers and walls between people?

4. When should children begin to buy their own clothes? How do children learn about quality, adaptability, comfort, and modesty?

5. Is it correct that men's clothing styles often show where they stand vocation-wise and status-wise?

6. How do you feel about the necessity to dress well because of one's position or status? Or dressing a certain way because one's job requires it? See entry page 108.

7. How much time and money is spent in your household on clothing purchase and maintenance? Include shopping, laundry, mending, and sewing. What percentages of homekeeping time and budget are taken up by clothing concerns?

8. Discuss and explore the "Do Justice" issues of buying cheap clothing made by underpaid workers.

9. How do you feel about hand-me-downs and garage sale or thrift shop clothing? How are such feelings generated? How can they be changed? What guidelines do you use for decisions of quality versus cost?

10. Aren't psychological needs to feel good about one's appearance, and to be attractive also important considerations? When is it okay to get something new in order to lift one's spirits? Is it okay to give away clothes when you are tired of them?

Action

1. For an icebreaker, have each person tell about something he or she is wearing. Describe your favorite article of clothing. Tell why you like it. Explain or show your best clothing buy to other members of your group.

2. Compare and contrast the advantages and disadvantages of various types of fabrics, such as cotton and wool versus polyester and dacron.

3. Sort and give away extra clothing you no longer wear. Change your buying habits in order to make clothes last longer and stay in fashion longer. Discuss ways to do this.

4. Demonstrate creative ways to dress up an "old" outfit. Display creatively mended or remade articles of clothing.

5. Have clothing exchanges in your group. Try this at your next family reunion, or set up a clothes closet at your church.

6. Refer to Herta Janzen's entry on page 105. Count the number of outfits you have hanging in your closet. A similar inventory can be made of magazines, books, and household cooking utensils, etc.

7. Investigate starting a pattern exchange at your public or church library.

8. Make a one piece shirt or a wrap around skirt, following the directions on page 112 and page 114.

9. Share ways you streamline the job of sorting and storing seasonal clothing. How do you lessen the time involved in clothing upkeep?

10. Note the principles on page 103. Add others to the list.

Resources

What Mennonites Believe About Clothes, Sue Steiner, Herald Press, 1980.

Beyond the Rat Race, Art Gish, Herald Press, 1973. Gives theory and suggestions, approaching clothes from the standpoint of overall lifestyle.

Scriptures

Dramatize the way Jacob used clothing to conceal his identity and get his way (Genesis 27).

Other stories where clothing figures prominently: Genesis 37, Matthew 17:2, 21:8, 27:35; Mark 14:52, 15:17; Luke 2:7; John 11:44, 13:3-5, 19:40; Acts 7:58; 9:32-43, 58, 16:14-15.

Jesus' words on clothing: Matthew 5:40, 6:28-34, 9:16, 20; 22:11; Mark 2:21, 12:38; Luke 5:36, 12:27-28, 15:22.

References to clothing in epistles and letters: Hebrews 1:11, James 5:2, 2 Timothy 4:13, Jude 23, Revelation 3

Session 9

Homes

Goals

1. To assess housing priorities such as location, size, and energy consumption.
2. To become aware of how rising expectations have affected housing decisions.
3. To be stimulated by exposure to creative ideas of homebuilding, such as solar energy, earth-sheltered design, shared living space.

Study

1. Why is there so much duplication of function in North American homes?

2. Why do we prefer single-family houses in suburbia or the country to living in condensed communities? What values are at work here?

3. Is it true that today's buildings keep us from encountering each other? See page 119.

4. What is the minimal space you could live with? How important is privacy and space to you? Do children need separate bedrooms? How can privacy be maintained in crowded, shared space?

5. What are the strengths and weaknesses of your present house? Are there any ways to make it more energy efficient?

6. Should we be more involved in securing decent housing for the homeless?

7. How much of our security is linked to where and how we live? Do childhood experiences play a large role in your housing expectations?

8. What do you think about the author's comments about controlling ourselves instead of trying to control the environment and the climate? Are we adapting to nature, or do we adapt nature to our needs? See pages 120 and 121.

9. When are the costs involved in energy retrofitting justified? What are the advantages and disadvantages of buying versus renting?

10. Is your house designed to nurture people? Are there ways you could improve its ability to nurture people? Does your house lend itself to hospitality?

Action

1. Discuss ways to invest less time, money, and pride in housing.

2. Have persons who have experienced extreme mobility share their feelings about home.

3. Leave water in the bathtub and dishpans, and vent electric dryers indoors for added heat and moisture in the winter.

4. Share personal experiences with energy savers like wood stoves, fireplaces, foil-backed drapery, insulation, heat grabbers, cross-ventilation windows, shade trees, solar heat.

5. Draw a floor diagram of your childhood home. What was your favorite room in the house? Why? What was the warmest room? The coldest room? Encourage your children to share their comments or do this exercise.

6. Write some principles for this chapter.

7. Share ways you have expanded your present space for maximum needs like extra company, the teenage years, and caring for elderly parents.

8. Examine rising expectations. Page 119 says the 1920 average house lot was 1/10 of an acre; today it is twice that. Recall how homes built in the 1950s differ considerably in size from those built in the 1970s. Have the group write down or discuss features they would like their homes to have if built in the 1980s.

9. Create a room or corner in your present house where solitude and beauty reign. Think of it as your worship center, or place where you cherish the natural order.

10. Make a list of the good and bad points of your present house and location. Evaluate them. If you don't own a house, make a list of your dreams—what you want in a house and location. See page 128.

11. Have persons who have lived in other cultures share differing concepts in housing. In Africa people live *around* a house, we live *in* a

house. Japanese have beds which can be stored in the closet so space is flexible; even a tiny one-room Japanese house would have some area reserved for beauty.

12. Plant some trees around your home. Contact your city planners with some facts, such as those given on page 121. Could your community be made 10 degrees cooler and use 50 percent less electricity for air conditioning by planting shade trees?

13. Respond to the entry on page 123. Share similar experiences of "Terrible Houses" that were fantastic!

14. Take a field trip in your community to see some creatively designed houses.

15. Write down five small steps you can take now to improve your existing housing arrangement. Write down five larger steps you would like to be able to take some time in the future.

16. Make a time line showing how man adapted to nature. Start with cave homes. Children will enjoy this activity.

17. Envision two days in the winter and two days in the summer without electrical power. How would your lifestyle be affected? What would you miss most? least?

Books

A House Is a House for Me, Mary Ann Hoberman, Viking, 1978.

Bokotola, Millard Fuller, Follett, 1977. Fascinating story of how the Koinonia community is involved in building low-cost housing in Georgia and Zaire.

Earth Sheltered Housing Design, Van Nostrand, 1978. Prepared by the underground space center, University of Minnesota.

The Owner-Built Home, Ken Kern, Scribner's, 1972. See especially chapter 3, "Ventilation," for a fascinating discussion of "climate control," and natural air conditioning.

Your Energy-Efficient Home, Floyd Hickok, Prentice-Hall, 1979.

Music

"This World Is Not My Home," well-known gospel song

Scriptures and Sermon Idea

Psalm 127:1	Luke 14:28-30
Matthew 7:24-27	Jeremiah 29:5
Luke 6:46-49	Haggai 1:4

Living in Tents—Hebrews 11:9, 10; Genesis 12:1-9

Session 10

Homekeeping

Goals

1. To make our homes sanctuaries where we highlight relationships over possessions and retreat from our noisy, overstimulating world.
2. To reduce dependence on commercial products for beautifying and cleaning.
3. To encourage recycling of glass, paper, aluminum, and composting of organic material.
4. To let meaning and function determine the look of objects, rooms, and yards.
5. To become more aware of wasteful energy consumption.

Study

1. How do we create space so that beauty and order can bloom in our modern, busy, come-and-go homes? What ways have you found to unclutter and organize your space? This may include ways you have found to streamline homekeeping tasks.

2. How do you use your living space wisely? Flexibly?

3. Should all members of the family be involved in homekeeping?

4. Is homekeeping an enjoyable part of your life? Why or why not? What are some ways you have found to make homekeeping tasks enjoyable?

5. What about the trade-offs of saving time and consuming energy in labor-saving devices? Do you have any guidelines to suggest for decisions about purchasing things like dishwashers, freezers, gas versus electric dryers?

6. What are your favorite ways of conserving water, fuel, and

energy? How much energy does your family waste? See the facts and figures on pages 49, 166-170.

7. Do you agree with Dr. Yoder's statement on page 49, "The most underutilized resource to aid in simple living is our own heads"? If so, what are some ways we could make better use of this resource?

Action

1. Make a list of the cleaning products and supplies in your house. Rank them. Which are the ones you cannot do without? Include personal products like toothpaste and deodorant also. One group listed 50 items in just a few minutes. If we only need ten, why do we use 50? Discuss the trade-offs in time, convenience, money.

2. Keep track of how much time it takes to keep things livable in your home. Compare notes. Make a breakdown of time spent in each of the following areas: laundry, cooking, and dishwashing, housecleaning, yard work, picking up/putting away, repairs and maintenance.

3. Evaluate your convenience and labor-saving devices. Consider questions like these:

—Do they enhance life?

—Is the time savings worth the pay-off in energy consumption?

—Do the devices control us?

—Do they deny creativity, rewards, and healthful activity of work?

—Are they offered as imitation love?

4. Share ideas for more orderly organization, planning schedules, family cooperation, housecleaning shortcuts. Share ways you have discovered to make repetitive homekeeping tasks more pleasant.

5. Give examples of beauty that blooms because it is framed in space.

6. Make banners, charts, or posters of the question: "Does it nurture people?" and "Does it protect our environment?" for display in your home, church, meeting place, and office.

7. Have each family make a list of everything in their home which uses energy. Count the light bulbs you have. Rank the lights and other items in order of importance. Which ones could you do without? Compare notes.

8. Wash all light globes; replace burned-out bulbs with smaller wattage bulbs where bright light is not needed for close work.

9. Share ideas for turning thermostats down, for increasing the

use of solar heat with and without reconstruction—such as hanging foil-back drapery, opening curtains, working in the room which has the most sunlight, closing off part of the house for the winter months.

10. If your local electric company does not list consumption of KWH on your bills, encourage them to do so. If it does, compare consumption within your group.

11. Report on monthly consumption of large appliances like freezers, air conditioners, dryers. Become aware of how much these appliances are costing you in dollars and cents, and in energy consumption. Share ways you have cut back and ways you share energy usage.

12. Using several women's, men's, or household magazines, *identify* articles and ads that are not based on more with less concepts. Underline key words such as pretty, clean, new, strong, luxurious, or their synonyms.

13. Demonstrate mixing your own cleaners. See page 150.

14. Take the ecology checkup in the Leader's Resource Section, page 100, if not used in session 5. Distribute copies to others.

15. Work in pairs or small groups to make brief television advertisements about the following products or opportunities. Act out the advertisements for the total group. As you share the advertisements, talk about the ways in which such advertisements influence our thinking and acting. How could advertisements be used for the public good? See page 130.

> —Make an advertisement which urges people to buy a new brand of tissue paper. Present it as softer, stronger, and cheaper than any other brand.
>
> —Make an advertisement which urges men to buy a new brand of deodorant which is supposed to make them irresistible to women.
>
> —Make an advertisement which urges people to conserve energy and to give the money saved to a world hunger cause.
>
> —Make an advertisement which urges people to vote in the next election and to consider the positions of candidates on the issues of world hunger and energy conservation.

Resources

Be sure to use the charts, pages 166-170 and the ecology checkup and song in the Leader's Resource Section, pages 99 and 100.

Only Silly People Waste, Norah Smaridge, Abingdon, 1973. Humorous verses about water, food, paper, electricity, shampoo, and other things children waste. Ages 5-99.

Hidden Art, Edith Schaeffer, Tyndale, 1971.

How to Clean Everything, Alma C. Moore, Simon and Schuster, 1971.

Scriptures

Luke 15:8-10—woman who swept her house to find a lost coin

Proverbs 31:10-31

Dramatize the Mary and Martha story, Luke 10:38-42.

Filmstrips

Beginning at Home, Teleketics, 1978, color, junior high-adult. Outlines ways in which energy can be saved by more efficient approaches to heating, cooling, and lighting. Urges viewers to stop being passive consumers and to live in such a way that all can live with dignity.

Holy Smoke: Biblical Reflections on the Energy Crisis, 1980, color, 30 minutes, junior high-adult. MCC, Akron, Pa. In the midst of confusion about the energy crisis, this filmstrip invites us to step back for a moment and examine the contributions our fundamental values can make toward understanding. Three great themes emerge: (1) the earth is good, (2) the earth is the Lord's, and (3) human beings exist to build the earth in partnership with God.

Session 11

Transportation and Travel

Goals
1. To consider ways to use our cars more efficiently and temperately.
2. To increase joy, pleasure, and purpose in vacation travel.
3. To consider alternate forms of transportation.

Study
1. What are some values of car pooling? What are some of the drawbacks? Why are so many people reluctant to car pool?

2. How have you used the word "no" to simplify your transportation needs?

3. When are long trips justified? Consider overseas trips, business trips, travel for education or recreation, as well as travel for visiting family and friends.

4. Why do you think Americans traveled twice as much in 1977 as they did a decade before? Will this ratio increase or decrease in the decade ahead? See pages 172-175.

5. What principles guide your decisions about local transportation and vacation travel?

6. Does your community have adequate public transportation? What could you do to support or increase existing resources for public transportation?

7. How have you pared down the list of take-along necessities when you travel? What are some of the obvious and less obvious advantages of traveling light?

8. What are some ways to balance spontaneity and planning on vacation trips?

Action

1. A fun ice breaker activity is to go around the circle completing one or more of the following: "When I travel I *always* take along. . . ." "I like to travel because. . . ." "I have traveled by . . . " (name modes of transportation, i.e. boat, train, bicycle).

2. Take the following quiz as an interest arouser for the chapter. Read it aloud and count the answers on your fingers to save paper! Find the answers on the pages listed. All are true except f.

True/False

a. More than one third of our travel involves visiting friends and relatives (p. 174).

b. More travel time is spent on business trips than on pleasure trips (p. 174).

c. Forty-five percent of all automobiles are found in North America (p. 173).

d. The U.S. has one car for every two persons (p. 173).

e. Transportation eats up 25.2 percent of the total commercial energy in the U.S. More than half this 25 percent is used by automobiles (pp. 170 and 173).

f. It is always best to buy a fuel-efficient car (p. 173).

g. Americans traveled twice as much in 1977 as they did the decade before (p. 172).

h. Lower speeds, slower starts, and gradual acceleration translate into significant fuel savings (p. 174).

i. Bus transportation gets the most passenger miles per gallon (p. 167).

j. Fuel economy is decreased 8.1 percent by driving 50 miles per hour rather than 40 miles per hour. It decreases an additional 11.3 percent at speeds of 60 miles and another 17.3 percent at 70 miles per hour.

3. Figure out how much you spend on transportation in an average year. Don't forget to include insurance costs. Compare figures with others in your group.

4. Visualize an oil embargo requiring North America to live on one half its present energy consumption. List and discuss what changes your family would make to reduce its consumption.

5. Volunteer to help each other with car maintenance jobs. Have a session where those experienced in car maintenance share their knowledge with others who lack expertise in this area.

6. Keep a log of miles traveled in one week or one month. Categorize the miles under business or work, errands, nurturing people, recreation. Or divide them into categories of miles driven, miles walked, miles shared—car pool or public transportation.

7. If there are persons in your group who do not have a car, have them tell how they manage without one. How can we decrease the use of automobiles?

8. Rewrite the parable of pulling down barns to build bigger ones so it applies to cars. See Luke 12:16-21 and the third entry on page 176.

9. Share favorite games or activities your family uses to make long car trips more enjoyable.

10. Make a collage of travel advertisements from a *Time* or *Newsweek* magazine. Count the number of travel ads in a single issue. Note how many are for big cars vs. smaller, more efficient cars and whether any other forms of travel other than private car are advertised.

11. Have someone in your group report on the vacation packages offered by the Church of the Saviour in Washington, D.C., which are purposely designed to expand the mind and heart, and to eliminate the divisions between the rich and poor. See *Letters to Scattered Pilgrims,* pages 24-26.

12. Do a Bible study on biblical themes of travel. Note concordance references under such words as journey, sojourn, sojourners, the way, wander, go, come, move, walk. Traveling is a major biblical theme. Recall Bible stories and events where traveling was important, i.e., the children of Israel in the wilderness, Abraham's journey, Jacob's journey, Naomi and Ruth, the Good Samaritan, Paul's missionary journeys, the journey to Jerusalem.

Bible Study or Sermon Ideas

Hospitality Along the Way—Matthew 10:5-15; Acts 28:14-16; Romans 15:24; 1 Corinthians 16:5-8; Deuteronomy 10:19

A Way, Not a Destination—Hebrews 11:8-10, 12:1, 2; John 14:6; Mark 8:34, 35; Isaiah 2:5; Psalm 25:4; Deuteronomy 5:33; 8:6

Music

"I'm Just a Poor Wayfarin' Stranger"—available in folk song collections.

Pamphlets

The Sacred Car, Faith and Life Press, Newton, KS. 67114

What Mennonites Believe About Cars, John Hershberger, Mennonite
   Publishing House, Scottdale, Pa. 15683.
Mennonite-Your-Way Directory, available from Box 1525, Salunga,
   Pa. 17538. Listing of nearly 2000 families throughout North
   America, and 60 contact persons in 40 foreign countries who have
   agreed to host travelers coming through their area.
The Christian on the Highway by Paul M. Lederach. A supplement to
   the National Safety Council defensive driving course. For in-
   formation write the Mennonite Publishing House, 616 Walnut
   Ave., Scottdale, Pa. 15683.

Audiovisuals
The High Price of Wheels, Teleketics, 1978, color filmstrip, junior high-
   adult. Asks timely questions about how to use a car in light of
   gasoline and oil shortages and danger to the environment. Public
   transporation, car pooling and routine maintenance are discussed.

Session 12

Celebrations

Goals
1. To reevaluate traditional ways of celebration.
2. To celebrate ways we are already living more with less.
3. To gain a better understanding of the real meaning and value of celebration and gift giving.
4. To share meaningful ways to celebrate without commercial consumption.
5. To encourage a more celebrative attitude in everyday life.

Study
    1. What is the purpose and value of celebration? How does celebration nurture people and strengthen faith?

    2. What are some guidelines for moderation and simplicity in celebration? How do we keep simplicity from becoming austerity?

    3. Harvey Cox says our rushed society, with its material drives and the self-conscious images we project, is losing its ability to celebrate. Guilt makes it hard to enjoy ourselves. How can we be freed from guilt and other feelings that diminish our ability to celebrate and live gratefully?

    4. What does celebration do for you? Is it restorative? Can you do it in isolation? What things did you celebrate today? What is your favorite kind of celebration? Why?

    5. Should every service of worship in a church be a celebration? What are some ways to make worship more celebrative?

    6. How can funerals be meaningful celebrations?

    7. How can you be considerate of the feelings of others who have

differing ideas of celebrations? For example, what are some ways to work with family gift exchanges that have become an albatross to some family members and priceless tradition to others?

8. When do you write letters? Do you find letter writing a good way to share yourself with others? Can a friendship be maintained or begun through correspondence?

Action

1. Share times when you have been able to separate celebrations from commercial interests. Give examples of gifts you have received or given that were gifts of love rather than something purchased.

2. Plan a celebration. Doris speaks mostly of weddings, birth, death, birthdays, Christmas, Halloween, and casual entertaining. Share some other events, days or traditions that you celebrate. See the Alternate Celebrations Calendar for some creative ideas of new holidays and new ways to celebrate. Place copies of the *Alternate Celebrations Catalogue* in your church and public libraries. The address is in the resource section.

3. Make a calendar for someone you love. Note the idea on page 202, or illustrate the months with your children's drawings, or photographs of events that took place in that month the previous year. Such calendars are priceless memories of family joys.

4. Create a display of original greeting cards and wrapping paper.

5. Save your Christmas cards and celebrate the friendships they represent. In the weeks that follow Christmas, choose one card each day to be remembered in prayers of thanksgiving and intercession. Treasure the gift of that person's friendship. Write a short letter or postcard to the sender.

6. Light a candle to celebrate the anniversary of a friend's or relative's death. Answering children's questions about "Why do you have a candle today?" can provide many meaningful times of celebrating, remembering, and cherishing the past.

7. Review and share some of the famous letter friendships, such as C. S. Lewis's *Letters to an American Lady,* Brother Lawrence, Emily Dickinson.

8. Get out some of the old letters you have saved. Reread and savor them. Show your children their first letter.

9. Write a birthday letter to your child on his/her special day each year. Include areas where you see growth taking place, problems, issues you and they are working on, special memories and highlights of

the year just past, comments about how the birthday was celebrated.

10. Find new ways to affirm the persons in your group. Celebrate and name each one's special contribution to your life together.

11. Make friends with one or two older persons who are lonely. Beautify their rooms. Give them something living to care for.

12. Lengthen rather than shorten holidays. For example, celebrate Advent and Twelfth Night, thus stretching Christmas celebrations from one big day to a month and a half of sharing joy. This helps create a broader focus beyond gifts and adds other traditions and meanings to Christmas.

13. Make every day a celebration of something—as you sit down to the evening meal or breakfast, try to think of something to celebrate. Ask, "What shall we celebrate today?" Include ordinary, local, historical and world events such as, the garden and yard are put to rest for the winter, Susan B. Anthony's birthday, a city bus system, peace in the Middle East.

14. Instead of giving newlyweds a head start in the business of acquiring things, make your next wedding gift an expression of gratitude, a promise of support, understanding, and encouragement.

15. When buying gifts for weddings, birthdays, and other special occasions, buy items which provide jobs and support poor people around the world, from MCC Self-Help (21 S. 12th Street, Akron, Pa. 17501) or from SERRV Program (Box 188, New Windsor, Md. 21776).

16. Do some advance planning for your funeral. Write your ideas down and share them with a family member.

Resources

Alternate Celebrations Catalogues, second, third, and fourth editions, and the *Alternate Celebrations Planning Calendar.* Order from Alternative Resource Center, Box 1707, 1124 Main St., Forest Park, Ga. 30050.

Family Nights Throughout the Year, Terry and Mimi Reilly, Abbey Press, 1978.

Celebration of Discipline, Richard J. Foster, Harper, 1978. Helpful discussion of inward, outward, and corporate disciplines that foster celebration and freedom.

A Time to Keep, The Tasha Tudor Book of Holidays, Rand McNally, 1977.

The Springs of Joy, Tasha Tudor, Rand McNally. Beautiful illustrations plus quotations and bits of poetry on the themes of celebration, nonconformity, personhood.

Music
"Lord of the Dance," 67, *Sing and Rejoice!*
"Christ Is Changing Everything," 16, *Sing and Rejoice!*
"Alabare," 4, *Sing and Rejoice!*
"Like David the Shepherd, I Sing," 59, *Sing and Rejoice!*

Audiovisuals
William, film available from United Methodist Communications, 1525 McGavock St., Nashville, Tenn. 37203, or your local library. Story of a picnic that is not much of a celebration for William.

Scriptures
Examine the meaning of celebration in: Matthew 11:16-19, Luke 12:19, 14:15-24, 15:20-32; Ecclesiastes 3:1-13, 9:7; Psalms 47, 66:1-4; 95:1-7, 149:1-5.

Session 13

Recreation

Goals

1. To avoid "burnout" and other symptoms of excessive work-related stress.
2. To reclaim zest for living and to keep the "child within" alive and well.
3. To help one another discover rhythms and priorities.
4. To claim the freedom to say "no" to good causes and frantic efforts to have "fun."

Study

　　1. Rhythm and change are more important than whether you work or have fun. What gives rhythm to your days and weeks? Do your children and your spouse experience rhythm and change? What could you do to give them a break?

　　2. How does our culture make us feel that time is money? Puzzle together over the paradox of Western society—for the first time man is free from having to slave every minute in order to eat, yet only a few appear to have rest.

　　3. What do you need to achieve *otium sanctum?* 'See pages 211, 212.

　　4. Which is easier for you—physical rest and relaxation, or spiritual renewal? Why? How does quiet time become a fixed habit? See entry on page 222. What adaptations of solitude and meditation work for parents of small children?

　　5. Is the ability to pace oneself learned? If so, what implications does this have for parenting?

　　6. How do you combat fatigue and time pressure? At work? At

home? Become aware of what fatigue does to you. How do you know when you are tired? How does fatigue affect your relationships with others?

7. Are you living now the way you honestly would like to live? If you knew you had only a year to live, what things would you change? Have someone who has faced this, or a recent illness, share how they reordered their priorities, and how quickly or slowly they reverted to a hassled existence.

8. What are some options to TV that work for you and your family? What modern forms of recreation or entertainment are most conducive to good living?

9. Are you too busy? What plan do you have for finding more leisure time for yourself and your family? What was the best vacation you have had in the past ten years?

Action

1. Give each pair a string to work with for five minutes, as a neat and easy way to begin the session. If you want to explore ancient string fun, see your public library. How many cat's cradles can you make?

2. Invite several older persons to tell how they had fun in their day. Ask them how they saved time without time- and labor-saving devices. Share new ideas for cooperative sports and games. See resources list.

3. Play hug tag. A player is safe from being tagged only when she or he is hugging another player. For more hugging, propose that only three persons hugging together are safe, then four, then five, and so on.

4. Try one of the games on pages 223-226. Perhaps "Dictionary" or "Who Did It?" will work best in a group setting. We call the former "Fictionary" since creative fibbing is part of it. This always proved hilarious when we played it, even in cross-cultural settings. It is a fun "after-dinner" game with guests you don't know very well.

5. Recreate together as a group. Picnic, go nutting, toboggan, or play volleyball.

6. Try fasting for one day. Covenant together to do this during the next week, then take time to share what your feelings and experiences were.

7. Have someone gather up all the Gospel readings about recreation and retreat and share a medley of these with your group, Mark 6:31-32; Luke 4:42; Mark 1:35.

8. Shivaree someone who has been married for a while, but needs

and can take a good joke. Make sure you bring the lunch along so when the couple invites you in you can celebrate.

9. Draw your childhood home, mark the favorite room, and the least favorite room. Repeat for the home you are presently living in. What made your childhood home attractive, restful, recreative? What does that in your present home? Pool insights and ideas here. Plan specific ways to make your home a more cheerful, happy, restful place.

10. List your children's favorite toys. Compare notes. Make a list of your favorite toys or recreational activities when you were a child. How does your list differ from that of your child? Are there joys from your childhood that you need to share with your children?

11. Spend an evening or afternoon with children and share some non-commercial toys, such as stilts, tin can walkers, a barrel hoop to roll, paper doll chains cut from newspapers, spool tatting, cat's cradles, spool tractors. Modern children have often never been exposed to such pleasures.

12. Sponsor a handmade toy fair at a local elementary school, shopping mall, church, or public library. This could take the form of a contest with age divisions and simple prizes, or it could be a bazaar with the profits going to some charitable cause. Its goal could be just exposure or an alternative to commercial Christmas gift buying.

13. Exchange with each other the ways you blur the distinction between work and recreation. How do you make dull work enjoyable?

14. Check yourself on the principles, pages 212, 213. Note in your journal the places where you are strong and the ways you need to improve. If number 6 is an issue for you, try to open up your needs by observing yourself.

15. Prepare a list of "Things Life Is Too Short For...." If you have access to Doris Longacre's list this could be used as a conclusion for this activity. ("Life Is Too Short," *Christian Living,* Apr. 1, 1980, page 14.)

16. Share ideas for mini-vacations and five-minute relaxers to use during the day. Do a group neck rub, place chairs in train fashion, pass the lotion and massage!

17. Try popping corn by candlelight! See page 221.

18. Share or demonstrate the ways you get physical exercise. If someone is acquainted with the aerobics movement, let them share its highlights.

19. Divide into small groups and work on some of the following: (1) Fun things that don't cost money. (2) Living by rhythms and

priorities—what are they? (3) What are some other ideas that work with small children (see page 228)? (4) Recreation ideas from the Bible. (5) Ways to blur work and recreation. (6) Making routines enjoyable.

20. Our daughter's orthodontist's office has simple scrapbooks of magazine cartoons pasted on pages of 9 x 12 paper stapled together. Make and donate a similar humorous book for your local doctor's or dentist's office.

21. Play a game. Distribute sheets of paper. Ask people to write the following words across the top of their page: *spools, detergent bottles, cardboard boxes, tin cans, string, paper*. Give the group five minutes to list recreation possibilities under each category. Award prizes for the largest number, the most creative idea, the most unlikely use, etc. Prizes should, of course, be something made of one of the items listed.

22. Compile a list of good read-aloud books, for adults as well as children. Some of my favorites are:

Cry the Beloved Country, Alan Paton, Scribners, 1961.

Henry's Red Sea, Barbara Smucker, Herald Press, 1965.

The Bronze Bow, Elizabeth Speare, Houghton Mifflin, 1961.

Little House series, Laura Ingalls Wilder, Harper, 1932.

Narnia Tales, C. S. Lewis, Macmillan, 1950.

I Met a Man, Houghton Mifflin, 1961. *You Read to Me, I'll Read to You,* Lippincott, 1961, *John J. Plenty and Fiddler Dan,* John Ciardi's Poetry books.

God's Trombones, James Weldon Johnson, Penguin, 1976

Hailstones and Halibut Bones, Mary O'Neill, Doubleday, 1961.

The Broken Chalice, Myron Augsburger, Herald Press, 1971.

Peace Be With You, Cornelia Lehn, Faith and Life, 1981.

23. Organize a quiet day retreat. Choose a restful setting, where people can find space to be alone. Prepare a brief meditation guide or have some input and inspiration, perhaps a time of singing together and sharing of favorite Scriptures. Then part for a couple of hours before returning to share briefly over a simple refreshment. Shared silence is the key, though most people need a theme or a few good questions to focus their thoughts. Encourage journaling, or writing prayers.

Some families have tried a variation of this at home—carry on the usual, but with as few words as possible (children have great fun reminding Mother and Dad!) or have a meal in silence occasionally. It's amazing how it recreates and how good the food tastes if you are not distracted by the usual bickering and conversation. Monasteries which have silent meals often have one person read aloud while the others eat—you may also want to experiment with this. The Psalms are a good choice, as is a continued story.

Sermon Topics and Scriptures
Exodus 20:8-11; Deuteronomy 5:12-15; Nehemiah 8:9-12; Isaiah 14:7; Lamentations 3:22-26; Ecclesiastes 3; Revelation 21; Mark 1:35; 6:31-32; Luke 4:42; Leviticus 23:3
Contemplate in Today's World?
How Does God Recreate?
Sabbath and Jubilee

Music
"Dear Lord and Father of Mankind," 274, *The Mennonite Hymnal*
"Lonesome Valley," 61, *Sing and Rejoice!*

Books
Gift from the Sea, Anne M. Lindbergh, Random, 1978.

Letters to Scattered Pilgrims, Elizabeth O'Connor, Harper, 1979. Read especially the chapter on Sabbath.

Fatigue and Time Pressure in the Modern Society, edited by Paul Tournier, John Knox, 1965.

Celebration of Discipline, Richard Foster, Harper and Row, 1978. Especially the chapters on celebration, fasting, solitude.

Pace of a Hen, Josephine M. Benton, Christian Education Press, 1961. Practical suggestions for balancing work, play, worship, and service.

Anatomy of an Illness by Norman Cousins, Norton, 1979. Discusses the role humor and laughter play in health.

Cooperative Sports and Games, Terry Orlick, Pantheon, 1978.

Peacemaking: Family Activities for Justice and Peace, J. Haessly, Paulist Press, 1980. See chapter 3 for many cooperative game ideas.

The New Games Book, Andrew Fluegelman, Headlands Press, Inc., 1976. Games in which aggression fades into laughter.

Ways to Play: Recreation Alternatives, James C. McCullagh, Rodale Press, 1978.

Children and Solitude, Elise Boulding, Pendle Hill Pamphlet #125, Wallingford, Pa. 19086.

Fun N Games, Rice, Rydberg and Yaconelli, Zondervan, 1977. Every game was chosen for its potential for contributing towards community.

Session 14

Meetinghouses

Goals

1. To see church buildings as tools to be used for mission rather than as monuments to God, the architect or the congregation.
2. To make more efficient and creative use of existing places of worship.
3. To channel giving into human needs rather than into expensive structures.
4. To recognize that contact with the neighborhood is important. God may want us to worship in the midst of poverty and oppression.

Study

1. What ideas and ways have you found to maximize your church building?

2. Why does such a strong sense of ownership often surface when flexible use of educational space is discussed? Some congregations experience this when the decision between pews or chairs is made. What are the hindrances to flexible use of various spaces in your meetinghouse?

3. Many persons resist using the church for community activities like recreation, tutoring, and day care. Why is so much emotion invested in such decisions? What are some positive ways to work with this kind of conflict in a congregation?

4. What are the values and purposes behind the symbolism and architecture of your church?

5. What are the necessary ingredients for beauty in meetinghouses?

6. Does your present meetinghouse have ample space for creative

movement, interpretative dance, and drama? Are these important?

7. How can you cherish the natural order of your present existing structure and building?

Action

1. Have an old-timer or even the architect (if available) come and tell your group the reasons for your building's structure and appearance. Find out the significance and meaning of your meetinghouse and its contents. For example, round churches often signify the fellowship of believers, a pulpit off to one side may be to show that the preacher is not central. Give other examples.

2. Journal about the different meetinghouses you have worshiped in.

3. Use the following quiz to arouse interest and enlarge awareness. Find the answers on the pages listed.

True/False

a. In 1975 Protestants in the U.S. and Canada spent ten times as much on church buildings as they gave to foreign missions (p. 231).

b. Current costs of facilities for Mennonite churches range from 30¢ to $1.00 for each use per person (p. 231).

c. In 1977 only one church out of 1,100 in Washington, D.C., responded favorably to a request for space for the city's homeless (p. 232).

d. The type of building or facility you have determines the quality of fellowship (p. 232).

e. Sharing church facilities is a new idea (p. 233).

f. Simplicity in church buildings usually means forfeiting beauty and elegance (p. 234).

g. This chapter calls for a moratorium on new church buildings (p. 230).

h. A church building should be a monument to God (p. 231).

i. By modifying its building program, a Presbyterian church was able to use the money to rebuild 26 churches and 28 pastor's houses destroyed by an earthquake in Guatemala (pp. 235, 236).

j. It is possible for a congregation to meet in two different locations and still coordinate activities (p. 236).

   (d, e, f, g, h are false, rest are true)

4. Take a tour of your present meetinghouse. Dream dreams and

see visions of ways its usefulness might be expanded. List all the present times and ways your building is used. Brainstorm about possible expansion of use.

5. Have an energy audit done on your meetinghouse. Plan ways to conserve energy. Don't forget no-cost possibilities like beginning services earlier in the summer months to lessen cooling costs.

6. Adapt your meetinghouse for handicapped persons.

7. Visit or explore other meetinghouses in your community which are strikingly different from yours. Find out whether form follows function. Quaker customs and house churches may be instructive for your group.

8. Write a prayer of dedication for your meetinghouse. Dedicate your meetinghouse to some new uses.

9. Case studies to analyze:

a. *The Paoli Church,* page 238, says they have four options. What counsel and suggestions do you have for this congregation? What principles or priorities should they use to make their decision?

b. *The Assembly in Goshen,* page 239, says they need a building of their own.

They see a church building as a place to meet *and* a place to use in response to community and world needs. How do you feel about their reasoning process? Can ministry be *the* most important criteria for a church building? Does having a building usually enhance ministry and reaching out in the community? Or does it do the opposite—stifle reaching out, by institutionalizing the church?

c. *The Reba Place Fellowship,* pages 239-240, enjoyed using their creative powers in designing and executing a building which met their needs in a fairly inexpensive way. What is the value of having the job done by professionals rather than members?

What are the trade-offs when you: (a) choose to do it yourselves? (b) choose to have professional expertise? What combinations of professional/lay involvement work best? When the members' powers are used in designing and executing your meetinghouse, does this make a difference in the level of commitment and ownership?

Resources

Local community architects and builders.

Minutes and history of your congregation, especially those items that relate to building decisions.

Varied past experiences of members in your congregation, especially the mobile ones who have worshiped in many different churches.

The Meetinghouse of God's People, Levi Miller, editor, Mennonite Publishing House, 1977.

The Energy Efficient Church, Total Environmental Action, Inc., by Douglas Hoffman. Pilgrim, NY, 1979

Scriptures
1 Chronicles 22; 28; 29
1 Kings 5-9, especially 8:27
Acts 6, and Acts 15, church decision-making

Music
"The Church's One Foundation," 375, *The Mennonite Hymnal*
"How Lovely Are Thy Dwellings Fair," 393, *The Mennonite Hymnal*
"To Thy Temple I Repair," 390, *The Mennonite Hymnal*

Session 15

Eating Together

Goals
1. To examine eating practices in light of *Living More with Less* standards.
2. To find new ways of enjoying and sharing hospitality.
3. To increase awareness of good nutrition and its importance.

Study
1. What are some principles for eating more with less?

2. How have we moved from an "eat to live" to a "live to eat" society? What is behind this kind of philosophy? How might we move again to an "eat to live" emphasis on healthful nutrition?

3. What ways have you found to avoid eating too much sugar, too much sodium, too much fat and cholesterol, too many calories?

4. What is the importance of nutrition in both causing and curing disease? What is the effect of nutrition on stress levels?

5. Are there times when fast foods are acceptable? Discuss what fast foods mean with regard to: energy use and resource waste, busy schedules, cost of food away from home.

6. What are your favorite ways of eating together? How can you multiply your capacity to have people in and your ability to respond with joy when they drop in?

7. Does simplifying company and holiday meals decrease the joy and pleasure of such occasions?

8. What are some other ways of giving homemakers recognition, other than complimenting their cooking ability? Why is there so much ego investment in our reputations as cooks and planners?

9. Do you agree that "being too busy to have you over" reflects immoral values? See page 254, last entry.

10. How do you feel about the trade-offs in time and energy consumption when you use paper table goods versus plates and cups that need to be washed?

Action

1. Demonstrate a time-saving, inexpensive, and convenient meal preparation, followed by a tasting party.

2. Fast one day a week to show solidarity with the hungry. Use what would be mealtime for prayer and study.

3. Working in small groups, draw up simple menus for a family reunion, a church conference, and a neighborhood birthday celebration. Plan for inexpensive but nourishing foods, using little preparation time, and sharing the workload. Write several samples on the chalkboard at the end of the project.

4. Make a list of biblical passages that deal with eating and drinking. Jesus has quite a lot to say about celebrating together over meals.

5. The author does not say much about the beverage issue. Share solutions you have found for drinkables:

—for large groups
—in light of "Do Justice" concerns, where coffee/tea plantations use farmland that could be used for food production
—health/nutrition concerns—sugared, colored drinks for children, caffeine and alcohol for adults
—the energy consumption of ice cold and steaming hot beverages
—for children who do not like milk

6. The standing food arrangement at First Mennonite Church in Iowa City is a "Bread-Cheese-Fruit Meal." Anyone brings whatever they want of those three items, just bread is fine, if that is all that is on hand, and when combined it makes a delightful, appetizing spread. Brainstorm other possibilities for finger food potlucks. See page 250.

7. Have a meal together. Usually it is a labor and time saver to have one or two persons cook in turn, rather than having the carry in type of meal where 10 or more persons end up spending time preparing the meal, and ten or more kitchens expend water and energy in the preparation.

8. Dream up other creative ways to eat together. Share favorite company meals that are easy on time, budget, and nutrition.

9. Make stone soup. Have each person bring one vegetable. Then

let the soup simmer while you talk about your eating habits. Children love this one, especially if someone brings three stones. (See *Stone Soup* listing on page 82 of this book.)

10. Try the salad picnic, page 267, where everyone signs up for one ingredient of tossed salad. So much easier and less sweet than the typical salad luncheon where everyone tries to outdo one another.

11. Eat an occasional shared meal in silence. It is amazing how much better the food tastes, and it enhances conversation at later mealtimes.

12. Share ways you have simplified family gatherings so there is more time for relationships.

13. Stages and places are important when entertaining guests. Share ways you have found to move the emphasis from the table and food to people and relationships. See both entries on page 254.

14. If you have any connections to an institutional dining hall (school, hospital, nursing home), try to introduce some of the Whitworth College concepts. Note that their experiment was optional and educational. See pages 256-257. The Whitworth idea has been adapted and used by many other private colleges, stressing "more not less."

15. Using the example on page 257, figure out how many paper cups your family or church uses in an average year. Explore the disposable cup issue at your local schools.

16. Make a display of paper cups and plates that are biodegradeable and those that are not. Figure out comparable costs.

17. Eat less with more style. You can serve smaller portions, and prepare a smaller number of different dishes, if you cook creatively and have more variety in what it is that you serve. There is no need, for example, to have a salad, vegetable, bread, jam, relishes, etc., with an international dish such as stir-fried green beans, *More-with-Less Cookbook*, page 221. The international dish is interesting enough in itself to not call for all the side dishes.

18. For one week, try to set the table with only the *needed* utensils. An Irish friend never washed unused silverware. She called them "Blessings" and returned them to the drawer.

19. Share memorable eating experiences. If persons in your group have lived in another culture or belong to one encourage them to share their observations.

20. For example, British friends seem to emphasize *how* you serve, rather than what is served. They make eating together an event which takes a whole evening, not a rushed affair over in an hour. A cold

drink, usually juice, is served in the living room before the meal, then you begin with light soup and bread, followed by a simple main course (small portions), then dessert, often bread pudding or fruit, then perhaps cheese and crackers, and finally small cups of hot tea or coffee in the living room—all interspersed with much conversation, and no haste. Very little meat needs to be served in this kind of meal, and much of the food can be prepared with little fuss. The hostess includes herself in the meal, and does not rush around trying to have everything on the table at once. You eat slowly, savor each course, and aren't tempted to take seconds and thirds—there usually are none—the host or hostess usually has all the plates at his/her place and serves you. It seems much more gracious and temperate than our home-style—reach and help yourself, there's plenty more in the kitchen.

21. Start a food co-op in your community if there is need for one. This is one good way to avoid wasteful packaging, and help provide nutritious foods and alternate protein sources at reasonable prices.

22. Read 1 Corinthians 11:17-34, then share communion together. This could take the form of a "Love Feast," traditional in Brethren churches, a simple meal of soup and bread or fruit, followed by the Eucharist, or simply share the bread and wine, serving each other.

Sermon Idea and Scriptures
Fasting or feasting? Isaiah 58:5; Isaiah 1:14; Matthew 6:16; 23:6; Leviticus 23:1-8 f.; Amos 5:21; Mark 2:19

1 Corinthians 11:17-34; Genesis 2:4-9; Philippians 3:17-21; Hebrews 13:1, 2; Luke 14:13; 1 Corinthians 3: 16, 17; Nehemiah 8:9-12; Revelation 21:17; John 21:12-14; 1 Corinthians 10:17; Proverbs 25:16; Mark 14:22-25; Acts 2:43-47; Matthew 25:35-40. Dramatize the parable in Luke 14:12-24.

Music
"Praise for Bread," 92, *Sing and Rejoice!*
"We Thank Thee, Lord, for This Our Food," 131, *Sing and Rejoice!*
"Let Us Break Bread Together," 55, *Sing and Rejoice!*
"Yours Is the Kingdom," 148, *Sing and Rejoice!*

Books
More-with-Less Cookbook by Doris Longacre, Herald Press, 1976. There is much helpful material on pages 1-52.

Loaves and Fishes: A "Love Your Neighbor" Cookbook, Linda Hunt, Marianne Frase, and Doris Liebert, Herald Press, 1980.

Open Heart: Open Home, Karen Mains, David C. Cook, 1976. The Life Response questions at the ends of the chapters are especially worthwhile.

Celebration of Discipline, Richard J. Foster, Harper, 1978. Especially chapters on celebration and fasting.

Stone Soup, Marcia Brown, Scribners.

The Empty Place, booklet available from Fransciscan Communications Center, 1229 South Santee Street, Los Angeles, CA 90015 has helpful awareness activities for families on food and hunger questions.

The Magic Cooking Pot, Faith Towle, Houghton Mifflin, 1975. Indian folktale which finds a way to feed the whole village.

Session 16

Strengthening Each Other

Good

1. To affirm and strengthen the steps families are taking in living more with less.
2. To help parents and children realize the joy and freedom in living more with less.
3. To explore specific ways of communicating simple living with children.

Study

1. Do you agree with Doris's list of the qualities our children need? See page 270.
   —A gentle way of handling the earth
   —Versatility in the face of shortage
   —Inner provision for contentment
   —Commitment to live justly in the kingdom of God

Can you add to her list, or amplify any of these four? Were you given this kind of legacy from your childhood? How do such qualities become part of our life's fabric?

2. How do you deprive creatively? Brainstorm on this one—share ideas, even if they seem far out. Newsprint or chalkboard listings may be helpful to stimulate creativity. Often one person's ideas will stimulate a related idea in another person.

3. Are poverty meals a negative or positive experience? What determining factors are at work here?

4. The text on pages 277-280 gives example after example of how other families involved children in some aspect of living more with less.

Can you make a similar list for your present situation? How do you encourage others and build convictions in your household? See also pages 271, 272.

5. What citizens' groups are already organized in your community? Do you have a food co-op or a garbage probe? A Citizens for Better Street Lighting? Parent-teacher associations? A hospice? Independent Living for Handicapped? Choose one of these community organizations where you might be able to contribute, or start some kind of organization to raise the consciousness of your community on matters which concern you.

6. How do you build a support group? How can your group become a caring, supporting community? Add to the following list:
—Measurable goals
—Hold each other accountable
—Covenant with each other
—Recognize your need for help
—Share honestly the struggles, conflicts, trade-offs
—Involve your entire family

7. It is interesting how Doris ended the book! Why do you think she placed those last two entries on obesity at the end of the book? How does obesity fit into this chapter? Perhaps one reason is that it often takes the support of a group to help persons control urges and change habits. Do you have other suggestions on how the book might have been drawn to a close?

Action

1. Find out how many in your group are dieting and why. Affirm those who are dieting. Have a successful dieter share how he or she reached goals. Add up the number of pounds overweight in your group; diet together. Consider the medical implications of extra pounds, by carrying a five- or ten-pound bucket of sand around with you for an hour. See entries on pages 285-286.

2. Share ways you yourself or others have lived creatively with affluence. See entry on page 282.

3. Divide into small groups of 3 or 4 and share past experiences when you received time as a gift from someone. See principle 6, page 271.

4. Calculate what your congregation could contribute to famine relief, in addition to tithes and offerings if all the members followed the Do Justice suggestion on p. 280.

5. If you have children, make a list of their friends, including adult friends. Star those who hold values similar to yours. If you do not have children, make a list of children whom you consider your friends.

6. Try in new ways to build a friendship relationship with one or two children.

7. Distribute magazines. Allow participants to find advertisements which encourage parents to indulge their children, i.e., give them all the advantages parents missed. Discuss.

8. If you know persons who have elected to live in community, invite them to speak to your group or plan a field trip to visit a nearby community. *Living Together in a World Falling Apart* has a list of communities complete with addresses and telephone numbers.

9. Check yourself by the principles on pages 271-272. Note places where you might improve.

10. Role play a parent-child interaction where simple living standards are caught. For example, a shopping trip, cooking a simple meal, a recreational activity.

11. Interview individuals who have experienced creative deprivation because of necessity, voluntarily, while living in another culture.

Scriptures
Colossians 1:9-11, Deuteronomy 6:4-9, Galatians 6:1-2, Romans 15:1-6.

Music
"Unity," 129, *Sing and Rejoice!*
"Fill My House," 24, *Sing and Rejoice!*
"The Joy of the Lord," 113, *Sing and Rejoice!*
" 'Tis the Gift to Be Simple," 128, *Sing and Rejoice!*

Books
Life Together, Dietrich Bonhoeffer, Harper, 1954. Especially chapters on community and ministry.
The New Community, Elizabeth O'Connor, Harper, 1976.
Beyond the Rat Race, Arthur G. Gish, Herald Press. Especially chapter 8.
Living Together in a World Falling Apart and *Coming Together,* Dave and Neta Jackson, Bethany Fellowship, 1978.

Session 17

Wrap-Up Session

Goals
1. To recognize that simple living is joyful, rich, and creative, but it is not simple. It requires work and change. See continuous self-evaluation as a source of vitality and strength.
2. To affirm and strengthen each other in the ways each has chosen to live more with less.
3. To encourage a perpetual response to God and each other in the areas of living standards. See living more with less as a process that never ends; it is an ongoing source of energy and direction.

Study
Many of these are a self-study; you may want to use some quiet time to work on them.

   1. What part of the study has been most meaningful to you? What has been least useful?

   2. What commitments have you made to living more with less?

   3. Where, in what areas, would you like to grow and change?

   4. What forms of resistance do you need to cope with in yourself and your situation?

   5. What are your values and priorities? How are you sharing these with others in your household? in your community?

   6. In which of the areas studied do you have the most questions, uncertainties, and reservations?

   7. Did your group become a support community for you as you attempted to make changes? How can you help others make changes?

   8. What reasons do you have at this time for making changes in

your life standards? How do these differ from those you had when your study group got started?

9. How do we avoid a swing back in the next generation? Is it easier for those not yet established, students, young-marrieds, to live more with less?

10. Do we agree that sufficiency (enough without excess or waste) and community (caring, sharing relationships) identify the direction of changes that need to be made today? Why so? How can more people be encouraged to move in this direction?

11. What is one visible project or action our group might undertake in our community to help create more awareness of the issues and concerns in this book? Do you know other persons who share similar concerns and goals?

12. What do you think of Elizabeth O'Connor's idea that in setting goals most of us project too much for one year, not enough for ten years?

Action

1. Have persons in the group read or refer to one of their favorite testimonies or quotations in the book, telling why they chose it.

2. Write down several goals or steps you plan to take in living more with less. Be specific. Talk about keeping a journal as a way to grow in living more with less. You can use a journal to write goals, observe self, and record feelings. When you meet your goals, affirm yourself. When you fail to meet goals, instead of judging and berating self, think back over the situations of the day to determine why. Compare self with self only, not with others. Revise unrealistic goals to intermediate steps. Learn to affirm success, forgive and forget failures—in oneself and others.

3. Have a living more with less celebration. This could take the form of a meal together, or bicycle trip, an outing, a living more with less fair or display, a field trip, a game or a film night.

4. In small groups invite participants to describe the situation surrounding a time of greatest happiness for them. Find common elements in such times. Do any of these reflect Doris's five standards outlined in *Living More with Less?*

5. Make a list of 10 things you would want to save if you suddenly learned your house was on fire. Reduce the list to five things. Number them in order of priority. Discuss what things were most important. What made them valuable?

6. Take each of the topics in Part 2 of the book, or a central focus like church, youth group, home, parenting. Have the group brainstorm ideas for change in this area. Then narrow it down to one recommendation that could be implemented and covenanted to do together.

7. Celebrate the things you are now presently doing. Write them down, name them, tell others about what you are already doing.

8. The final entries on pages 287 and 288 seem particularly cogent. Is it an open-ended book, as Doris had hoped it would be, a stimulus to more stories?

9. Provide paper and pencil for persons to create their own response to the book. Ask participants to write down new things they have tried, problems they have encountered in their search for ways to live more with less.

10. Incorporate your concern in already existing groups. For example, have your Bible study or small group spend one evening writing letters to newspapers, congressmen, local organizations.

11. Evaluate your church programs using the life standards in Part 1. Consider having a small group to represent each of the five life standards. Each group should consciously enact and be responsible for issues and concerns relating to their life standard. They could become, as it were, a conscience for the wider group, keeping concerns in that area alive.

12. Stress the fact that we have political freedom to speak and act and change. Those people in the oppressive regimes do not have that power. So we must speak out for them.

13. What you do with free time is an important summary question. Keep track of how you spend your time for one week. Are any measurable portions of your time spent in doing justice, learning from the world community, or cherishing the natural order?

14. Close your eyes and relax. Imagine you've just been told that you have a limited amount of time before you will die. How do you feel about this? What changes will you make in your present schedule and lifestyle in order to use the remaining time for the most important things? After a few minutes, open your eyes and share your experience with your partner.

15. Following the reading of several Bible passages on use of time and money, separate individually for 10-15 minutes for silent meditation on what God has to say about priorities. Share the resulting insights in groups of four.

16. Select one or two areas of change to which you are willing to

commit yourself personally or as a group (even for as short a time as one week). Make a list of what you can do, will do, and are currently doing. Share your responses with the group. Are there projects which you would like to do as a group? (See page 92.)

17. Pray daily for the poor and hungry of the world, for overseas workers, for community volunteers, for government leaders. Pray that your family and the church may grow in sensitivity to the needs of the world and find creative ways to minister in the Name of Christ.

18. Christian education ought to lead into mission. Plan some kind of community involvement beyond the congregation that would perform a valuable mission in the community. For example, start a food co-op, petition for bike paths and public transportation, set up a food pantry for hungry persons in your community, provide a van or housing repair service for elderly persons, investigate starting a hospice.

19. Read the Shakertown Pledge, page 104, in the Leader's Resource Section and ask for people to freely sign it.

20. Use the summary checklist and worksheet in the Leader's Resource Section, pages 102-104

Books

Food First, Frances Moore Lappé and Joseph Collins, Ballantine paperbacks, 1979. See especially the introductory materials, chapter 50, "What Can We Do?" and Appendix A, "Organizing for Change."

Help Me to Adapt, Lord, Judith Mattison, Augsburg, 1981. Seventy-five prayer conversations on adjusting your living standard to changing times.

Politics of Jesus, John Howard Yoder, Eerdman's, 1974. See especially page 65 for a discussion of "Jubilee."

The Graduated Tithe, Ronald J. Sider, InterVarsity, 1978 has a checklist of practical suggestions, page 24-27.

Recommended Study Guides for Further Study

See the Leaders Resource Section for recommended study guides for further study.

Music

"Christ Is Changing Everything," 16, *Sing and Rejoice!*
"Be Thou My Vision," 300, *The Mennonite Hymnal*
"Yours Is the Kingdom," 148, *Sing and Rejoice!*

Sermon Ideas
The Secret of Contentment, Philippians 4:11-13
Journey Inward, Journey Outward, Matthew 12:33-35; 15:14-20; Mark
    7:14-20

Scriptures
Philippians 2:4; 4:11-13
Luke 12:22-31, 54, 55
Leviticus 25

Prayer
"Deny us ease, but give us the glory of compassion."—Barbara Reber

LIVING
MORE WITH LESS

Leader's Resource Section

1. Projects: Small, Medium, and Large

(For Use with Session 1 and 17)

Small Living-More-with-Less Steps

1. Recycle newspapers.
2. Place copies of *More-with-Less Cookbook* and *Living More with Less* in local dentists' or doctors' offices.
3. Charge yourself a "tax" on imported foods and give it to an agency working toward justice for peasant farmers.
4. Put up and use a clothesline.
5. Avoid excess packaging and instant foods.
6. Subscribe to *Sojourners, Bread for the World Newsletter,* or *The Other Side* for yourself and a church leader.
7. Write a letter to the editor of your local paper to protest high taxes for defense spending in a hungry world.
8. Send a day's wages to an organization working for peace and justice.
9. Ask your pastor to preach a sermon on living more with less, and dialogue with others in the congregation after he does.
10. Ask six people if they know what percentage of their federal tax dollar is used for defense-related spending.

Medium Living-More-wtih-Less Steps

1. Increase giving to your local church or mission and service causes by 5%.
2. Keep a record of all expenditures. Find out where your money goes.
3. Plan an audiovisual evening on voluntary simplicity.
4. Share appliances.
5. Carpool and encourage others to do the same.
6. Invest in some form of solar energy conversion.
7. Fast one day per week.
8. Secure the commitment of five persons to visit or write letters to government officials on behalf of someone who is suffering injustice.
9. If it is under a mile, begin walking to church, or friend's house.
10. Develop a friendship with a third world person.

Large Living-More-with-Less Steps

1. Establish a land concerns group.
2. Create a volunteer or low cost repair service for senior citizens.
3. Adopt the graduated income tithe. (*Rich Christians,* p. 175-178)
4. Start a food co-op.
5. Plan a workshop for neighborhood and church people on the need for living a more simple lifestyle.
6. Sell your second (or first) car and give to the poor (Luke 12:33).
7. Change your employment to work which contributes more to human health and survival and less to luxury and destruction or take a job you enjoy more even though it may pay less.
8. Initiate alternative Christmas celebrations in your family and neighborhood.
9. Spend your next vacation with a Christian family in a cultural or economic milieu different from your own.
10. Do what you feel is just even though it may cost you friends, a job, or security.

2. Motivation Quiz

(For Use with Sessions 1 or 2)

1. Which of the following statements best describes you?
    __ I want to change my style of life, but need more affirmation.
    __ I feel comfortable with my style of life presently, which is about average for USA.
    __ I feel terribly burdened by my participation in an unjust system.
    __ I need a conversion in my lifestyle.
    __ I need to feel joy in simple living.
    __ I feel there is no virtue in living a simple lifestyle—it just makes life more complicated!

2. I first became interested in simple living because of—
    a) Values held by my parents

b) Values held by my peers
c) An increased understanding of the world situation
d) Becoming disillusioned with materialism

e) Other _____

f) I'm not interested in a simple style of life

3. Overpopulation is a world problem. Which countries have more
   people per square mile:
   Great Britain or India?
   Italy or Pakistan?
   Netherlands or China?
   West Germany or Philippines?   *Rich Christians*, page 53

4. The USA promotes grain exports mainly
   a) To help feed hungry people
   b) To other industrialized nations
   c) To balance our oil trade deficit   *Farming the Lord's Land*, page 16

5. The USA is more generous in foreign aid than most other
   developed nations. True or False?   *Rich Christians*, page 51

6. The USA spent (5) (24) or (42) times more on
   defense than on non-military aid in 1975.   *Rich Christians*, page 52

7. Of all the automobiles in the world (45%) (25%)
   or (15%) are in North America.   *Living More with Less*, page 173

8. The USA (bread basket of the world) produces
   (52%) (27%) or (13%) of the annual grain
   production of the world.   *Farming the Lord's Land*, page 14

9. The USA is the largest importer of beef. True or false?
                                              Rich Christians, page 159

10. Capital flow is four times greater from
    a) USA to Latin America
    b) Latin America to USA   *Rich Christians*, page 161

11. Japan uses about (⅓) (½) (⅔) as much energy
    per capita as the U.S.A.   *Living More with Less,* page 166

—Quiz prepared by
Ken Gingerich
Iowa City, Iowa

Let group find answers in resources quoted:
   Rich Christians in an Age of Hunger: A Biblical Study by Ronald J. Sider, Inter-Varsity Press, 1977.
   Farming the Lord's Land: Christian Perspectives on American Agriculture by Charles P. Lutz, Augsburg, 1980.
   Living More with Less by Doris Janzen Longacre, Herald Press, 1980.
   The answers are: 3. Great Britain, Italy, Netherlands, West Germany! 4. (b); 5. False; 6.42; 7. 45%; 8. 13%; 9. True; 10. (b); 11. (⅓).

3. A Choric: More Is Less/Less Is More

(For Use with Any Session)

Arrange two groups of both men and women, mounted on risers on each side of the stage. Lighting may be used for emphasis. Group 1 begins; Group 2 answers.

Group 1	Group 2
More is less.	Less is more?
(Louder) Less is more.	*(Louder)* More is less?
More with less is not a slogan—it is a glimmer of hope for disciples of Jesus in an unjust world.	*(Defiantly)* Injustice is a deceptive term to cover up laziness and lack of initiative.... God helps those who help themselves.
Truth comes only to those who must have it, who want it badly enough. And gifts of healing come only to those willing to change.	We are tired of being asked to change, of being made to feel guilty for the blessings God has given to us.
The gospel is a message of change; we are continually in need of being transformed.	But God has shown His favor by blessing us materially.

Wealth is more a matter of responsibility than a reward for faithfulness. "If anyone has material possessions and sees his brother in need but has no pity on him, how can the love of God be in him?"

We *do* share with others by tithing. We have worked hard for what we own, and God expects us to enjoy the fruit of our labor.

"Love the Lord your God with all your heart and with all your soul and with all your mind. Love your neighbor as yourself."

When our profits show a yearly increase, that is only good business. We are utilizing the abilities and talents given to us by God.

"How hard it is for the rich to enter the kingdom of God. Indeed it is easier for a camel to go through the eye of a needle than for a rich man to enter the kingdom of God. Sell everything you have and give to the poor, and you will have treasure in heaven."

But I have financial obligations, children to feed and clothe, a family to support. . . .

"Any of you who does not give up everything, cannot be my disciple. . . . A person's life does not consist in the abundance of possessions. . . . Where your treasure is, there will your heart be also. . . . Seek first my kingdom."

Our society tells us that *more* brings happiness. How do we overcome pressures to succeed and to consume?

Growth always involves some pain, some stretching and changing.

How do we begin?

If you head into unfamiliar woods, you had better find companions first; if you want to buck traffic, organize a convoy. To nonconform freely, we must strengthen each other.

But how do we know which way to go?

There is hope for us but no easy answers. There is truth but never without a search.

Who will teach us?

Female voice: The Holy Spirit will instruct us as we seek to be sensitive to the hurts of others, hurts we may have never experienced ourselves.

Male voice: We can learn from the world community. The best reason for listening to and learning from the poor is that this is one way God is revealed to us.

Female voice: We can be nurtured by one another in the Christian community, helping each other to determine priorities, identifying what is good so that our souls may live.

All voices: True evangelical faith cannot lie dormant.

It clothes the naked.	It serves those that harm it.
It feeds the hungry.	It binds up that which is wounded.
It comforts the sorrowful.	It has become all things to all men.
It shelters the destitute.	

Male voice: Jesus spoke more about the seduction of wealth than he did about prayer. Both the Old and New Testaments speak to the issues of doing justice, of being a people of shalom who care about a person's total well-being.

Female voice: How then shall we do justice, love kindness and walk humbly with our God?

All men: We will repent of our greed, of our tendency to buy and use more than is necessary. We will believe that the less we need, the freer we become.

All women: We will listen to our brothers and sisters when they speak about our overconsumption.

All men: People will have priority over our possessions. We will reduce our wants and share what we have as one contribution to world peace.

All women: We will realize that the bread in our cupboards belongs to the hungry man; the coat hanging unused in our closets belongs to the person who needs it; our shoes rotting from disuse belong to the one who has no shoes; the money we hoard belongs to the poor.

All men: We will find joy in serving rather than in being served, in using less ourselves so that we will have more to share.

All women: Instead of depending on our homes, our bank accounts, and our insurance policies, our faith in Jesus Christ will provide our hope and security.

All men: We will live more simply, not because the results will be immediate, but because living in this manner is right and good.

All women: We will make a peace treaty with nature by conserving the earth's resources. We will act as caretakers rather than as owners.

All men: We will be ready to make the bigger changes in our living patterns which grow out of simple acts of cutting back.

All women: We will believe that our efforts to live simply can encourage others to do the same.

All voices: Lord Jesus, take away our selfishness.
            Guide our choices.
            Give us the courage and wisdom to be faithful.   *Amen*

—Written by Sara Lou Wengerd,
    compiled from *Living More with Less*

4. A Reading: Body and Bread

(For Use with Session 3)

Leader: I am the bread of life, says the Lord. The one who comes to me shall not hunger (John 6:35).

People: He is the bread of life; I shall not want (Psalm 23:1).

Leader: This is my body, says the Lord, broken for you (1 Corinthians 11:24).

People: His body is bread, broken for us.

Leader: You are the body of Christ.

People: We are his body.

Leader: His body is bread.

People: We are Bread.

Leader: His body is broken.

People: We are broken.

Leader: His body is the bread which he gives for the life of the world (John 6:51).

People: We are his body. We are broken. We are bread for the world.

All: ALLELUIA!

—Reprinted by permission of Bread for the World from *The Challenge of World Hunger,* a study guide to the Preliminary Report of the Presidential Commission on World Hunger.

5. Song: Let's Take Care of God's Good Earth

(For Use with Sessions 5 and 10)

Tune: "Jesus Loves Me"

1. Let's take care of God's good earth.
Water, forests, air, and soil.
Don't toss out that used tinfoil.
Ride your bike and don't burn oil.
Love one another,
Share with each other,
Save this great earth of ours,
and learn to do with less.

2. Buy the things you really need.
Learn to enjoy the simply things.
Do a hobby, play some games;
Eat at home, invite some friends.

(repeat chorus)

3. Take care where you spend your cash.
Wear used clothing, mend your rips.
Put more in the offering plate.
Help poor people with their fate.

(repeat chorus)

—*Monica Honn, Rachel and Ingrid Friesen, Noreen Gingerich*

6. An Ecology Checkup

(For Use with Sessions 5 and 10)

I can't	I don't want to	I might	I'll do it sometimes	Easy. I'll do it	
					walk instead of asking for a ride
					ride a bike instead of asking for a ride
					help to organize car pools
					ask drivers to use unleaded gas
					throw papers in trash cans
					use dishes instead of paper plates, reuseable cups instead of paper cups
					save newspapers for recycling
					use the backs of writing and drawing paper
					save envelopes and wrapping paper to use again
					ask your school to buy recycled paper
					save cans and bottles for recycling
					use plastic bags over and over
					avoid buying things in plastic containers or wrappers
					turn off all water faucets tightly
					fix drips and leaks
					don't let water keep running when you brush your teeth
					run dishwashers and washing machines with full loads only
					don't use the toilet as a wastebasket
					turn off lights when you're not using them
					put garbage into a compost pile
					plant trees
					fix things instead of throwing them out
					save parts from old bikes to fix new ones
					give outgrown clothes to someone smaller
					share books, games, magazines with your friends
					talk to people about ecology
					add things to this list and make copies for other people

—From *Save the Earth: An Ecology Handbook for Kids,* by Betty Miles, Copyright © 1974 by Betty Miles. Reprinted by permission of Alfred A. Knopf, Inc.

7. Suggestions for a Self-Imposed Luxury Tax

(For Use with Session 2 or 7)

We are interconnected with others around the world. A voluntary self-imposed luxury tax is just one way of increasing our awareness of this interconnectedness of our lives and the lives of the poor. It is a tool we can use to examine our overconsumption of the world's resources and begin to bring our lives into line with a biblically just world economic order.

A self-imposed luxury tax recognizes that our high level of consumption is one reason many people are still poor in the world. The tax is a symbolic way of demonstrating our willingness to pay fair prices and wages to poor people who make our affluence possible.

With the money that *we save by taxing* our luxuries *or by foregoing luxuries altogether,* we can then *give more* to our church agencies who are working in relief, development, and justice programs around the world. Donate your luxury tax to MCC, or some other agency which is seeking to promote justice for underpaid workers.

Following are four suggested options for taxing yourself:

1. Tax yourself the same amount as your state sales tax.

2. Following the biblical idea of tithing, tax yourself 10% of the retail price of the item.

3. Use a tax comparable to the percentage of the specific luxury that you use that is imported. For instance, since one third of all strawberries sold in this country are imported, tax yourself 33% on all out-of-season strawberries that you buy.

4. In many countries, imported items are charged 100% duty. If you are ready for a radical step, use your purchase price as your self-imposed tax.

Here are some suggested items to be taxed:

1. Levy a tax on all imported food items such as fish, coffee, tea, spices, sugar, and out-of-season imported vegetables and fruits.

2. Tax yourself on manufactured goods that use raw materials and metals from poor countries and that are often mined by poor people.

3. If you don't recycle, tax yourself on your use of aluminum and plastic packaging containers that use imported metals and scarce petroleum products.

4. Tax your gas bill for gas used on nonessential driving such as recreation, vacation travel, and extra trips to the store.

5. Tax yourself on all pet food that you purchase.

6. Tax yourself 25¢ per month for every pound you are overweight.

7. Every year at income tax time, tax yourself $25 for every $1,000 you make above the poverty level. This level in 1980 was $7,450 for a non-farm family of four.

8. Tax yourself on clothing items that are imported and sewn by underpaid Asian workers.

9. Tax yourself on convenience items that use natural resources, such as paper towels, aluminum foil, tissues, sandwich bags.

—From Hunger Packet, MCC MILLINDO Food and Hunger Office, Route 2, Box 79, North Manchester, Ind. 46962.

8. Summary Work Sheet for Concluding Activity

(For Use with Session 17)

1. List all the things which you feel you need but don't have.

2. Who or what stands in the way of your having these needs met?

3. List below those things that you want and/or have but do not feel you need.

4. If you choose to eliminate these things from your life, who or what stands in the way?

5. Study this list of possibilities for conserving and saving (including various possibilities in addition to the elimination of things). Check several items that offer the best possibilities for changes in your lifestyle.

a) Using things less and/or longer (including emphasis on maintenance and repair):

____Cars   ____Furniture   ____Books/Papers
____Appliances   ____Clothing   ____Other:

b) Recycling:

____Paper   ____Bottles   ____Plastic
____Cans   ____Toys   ____Other:

c) Changes in eating habits:

____Less meat (especially when produced from grain)
____Less use of packaging
____Avoidance of waste
____More attention to nutrition   ____Other:

d) Alternative transportation:

____Walking   ____Car Pool
____Bicycling   ____Public transportation

e) Efficiency and frugality in:

____Heating   ____Insulating   ____Water Use
____Cooling   ____Cooking   ____Other:

f) Production for home consumption:

____Gardening   ____Freezing   ____Construction
____Canning   ____Sewing   ____Other:

g) Organic methods of lawn care and gardening:

_____Lawn care (e.g., less chemical fertilizer and watering)

_____Gardening (organic fertilizer, composting, mulching, etc.)

6. What (if any) specific change(s) do you choose to initiate this week?

—Adapted from *A Covenant Group for Lifestyle Assessment,* by William E. Gibson

9. The Shakertown Pledge
(For Use with Session 17)

Recognizing that the earth and the fullness thereof is a gift from our gracious God, and that we are called to cherish, nurture, and provide loving stewardship for the earth's resources,
And recognizing that life is a gift, and a call to responsibility, joy, and celebration, I make the following declarations:

1. I declare myself to be a world citizen.
2. I commit myself to lead an ecologically sound life.
3. I commit myself to lead a life of creative simplicity and to share my personal wealth with the world's poor.
4. I commit myself to join with others in reshaping institutions in order to bring about a more just global society in which each person has full access to the needed resources for their physical, emotional, intellectual, and spiritual growth.
5. I commit myself to occupational accountability, and in so doing I will seek to avoid the creation of products which cause harm to others.
6. I affirm the gift of my body, and commit myself to its proper nourishment and physical well-being.
7. I commit myself to examine continually my relations with others, and to attempt to relate honestly, morally, and lovingly to those around me.

8. I commit myself to personal renewal through prayer, meditation, and study.
9. I commit myself to responsible participation in a community of faith.

10. Reasons for Choosing a Simpler Lifestyle

(For Use with Any Session)

Today's global realities call for comfortable Christians to review their lifestyles. Guidelines for a simpler style of life cannot be laid down in universal rules; they must be developed by individuals and communities according to their own imagination and situation. A simpler lifestyle is not a panacea. It may be embarked upon for the *wrong* reasons, e.g., out of guilt, as a substitute for political action, or in a quest for moral purity. But it can also be meaningful and significant in some or all of the following ways:

1. As an *act of faith* performed for the sake of personal integrity and as an expression of a personal commitment to a more equitable distribution of the world's resources.
2. As an *act of self-defense* against the mind-and body-polluting effects of overconsumption.
3. As an *act of withdrawal* from the achievement-neurosis of our high-pressure, materialist societies.
4. As an *act of solidarity* with the majority of humankind, which has *no choice* about lifestyle.
5. As an *act of sharing* with others what has been given to us, or of returning what was usurped by us through unjust social and economic structures.
6. As an *act of celebration* of the riches found in creativity, spirituality, and community with others, rather than in mindless materialism.
7. As an *act of provocation* (ostentatious *under*-consumption) to arouse curiosity leading to dialogue with others about affluence, alienation, poverty and social injustice.
8. As an *act of anticipation* of the era when the self-confidence and

assertiveness of the underprivileged forces new power relationships and new patterns of resource allocation upon us.

9. As an *act of advocacy* of legislated changes in present patterns of production and consumption, in the direction of a new international economic order.

10. As an *exercise of purchasing power* to redirect production away from the satisfaction of artificially created wants, toward the supplying of goods and services that meet genuine social needs.

The adoption of a simpler lifestyle is meaningful and justifiable for any or all of the above reasons alone, regardless of whether it benefits the underprivileged. Demands for "proof of effectiveness" in helping the poor simply bear witness to the myth that "they the poor" are the problem and "we the rich" have the solution. Yet, if adopted on a large scale, a simpler lifestyle will have significant socio-political side effects born in the rich and in the poor parts of the world. The two most important side effects are likely to be economic and structural adjustments and release of new resources and energies for social change.

—By *Jorgen Lissner,*
Lutheran World Federation

*   *   *

The government (The Center for Science in the Public Interest in Washington, D.C.) has suggested the following reasons for living simply:

*Naturalistic—helps us appreciate the serenity of nature, its silence, the changes of season, and its creatures.

*Symbolic—promotes solidarity with the world's poor, and reduces the hypocrisy of our current overconsumptive lifestyle.

*Person-Oriented—affords greater opportunities to work together and share resources with one's neighbors.

*Ecological—reduces our use of resources, lessens pollution, and creates an awareness that we must live in harmony with our world.

*Health—lessens tension and anxiety, encourages more rest and relaxation, reduces the use of harmful chemicals, creates inner harmony.

*Social—induces frustration with the limited scope of individual action and incites us to move to social and political action levels.

*Economic—saves money, reduces the need to work long hours, increases both number and quality of jobs.

Spiritual—allows time for meditation and prayer, and rejects materialistic values.

—From *99 Ways to a Simple Lifestyle*
The Center For Science in the Public Interest
Washington, D.C.

11. Resources for Teaching

Recommended Study Guides for Further Study

Visions of a World Hungry, Thomas Pettepiece, Upper Room, 1978. Excellent devotional resource to further stimulate thought and commitment.

Simple Living. The Brethren Press, Elgin, Ill., 1974. See especially pages 33, 34.

Repairing Your Lifestyle, Clapp, Brownfield, and Siebert. Though intended for youth groups, it has good journaling-observing exercises for anyone wishing to go deeper. Write to: Council on Ministries, 1211 North Park, P. O. Box 2050, Bloomington, Ill. 61701. Ask also for their C-4 Journaling Resource. *Repairing Your Lifestyle* can be a helpful resource for programs, service projects, parties, and fund-raising events even if you don't do a systematic study.

A Covenant Group for Lifestyle Assessment, William E. Gibson, Jacksonville, Fla., Convention Press, 1978. Useful guide for groups serious about living more responsibly. Twelve session outlines include activities as well as study and discussion. Order from United Presbyterian Church U.S.A., Social Education Office, 475 Riverside Dr. Room 1101, New York, N.Y. 10027.

Hunger Activities for Children, Brethren House Ministries. St. Petersburg, Fla., 1978. Introduces hunger issues through Bible learning, arts and crafts, games, music, and writing. Adapts to a variety of ages.

Creative Food Experiences for Children, Mary T. Goodwin and Gerry Pollen. Center for Science in the Public Interest, 1974. Activity and information book for leaders and teachers of children from preschool on up. Teaches basics of good nutrition and consumption with fun activities.

Educating for Peace and Justice. A Resource for Teachers, Institute for Education in Peace and Justice, 3700 West Pine, St. Louis, Mo. 63108. A curriculum for teaching about peace, justice, economics, hunger, military, for public and religious schools.

Focusing on Global Poverty and Development, Jayne C. Millar, Overseas Development Council, 1974. A resource book for teachers of older elementary, secondary and college students on all aspects of the hunger/justice issue.

Food: Where Nutrition, Politics and Culture Meet, Katz, et al., CSPI, 1976. An activity book for teachers of children of all ages on eating patterns, nutrition, food consumption and supply, global and domestic hunger.

Have You Ever Been Hungry? Kutzner, Patricia L., and Stoerkel, Linda. New York: United Church Press, 1978. A six-chapter school curriculum guide for grades 3-4, 5-6, 7-8, introducing children to world hunger. Stresses awareness of nutritional needs and creates an appreciation for the food habits of other cultures. Order from United Church Board for Homeland Ministries, Division of Publication, 132 W. 31st, New York, N.Y. 10001.

MCC Resource Catalog, a listing of audiovisual and printed materials, 1980-81. This is a free-loan audiovisual library; you pay only the return postage. Order at least 3 or 4 months in advance to insure that you receive the materials you request. See addresses under "Workshop Resources" below.

Things That Make for Peace: A Personal Search for a New Way of life. Schramm, John and Mary. Minn: Augsburg Publishing House, 1976. Experiences and reflections which explore the issues of nonviolence, ecology, world hunger, contemplation, and personal relationships to help the reader create a more peaceful way of life.

Voluntary Simplicity: Study/Action Guide. Smith-Durland, Eugenia. Jackson, Miss: Convention Press, 1978. A twelve-session small group resource which probes New Testament teaching for direction on celebrations, simpler living and justice. Prepared for *Alternatives.*

Hunger: Understanding the Crisis Through Games, Dramas and Songs. Sprinkle, Patricia. John Knox Press, 1980. The games, skits, songs, and other resources in this book provide all age-groups the opportunity to explore worldwide concern with hunger. Schools, church groups, youth departments, and adults will find materials to fit any size group and time period. Bible games, fact-finding games, lifestyle evaluations, songs for worship and fun, experiential activities, programs involving food settings.

World Hunger, A Unit for Teachers, 1976. Institute for Education in Peace and Justice, 1976. A short, but effective list of classroom activities for action pertinent to younger students.

Periodicals

Alternatives: A Voluntary Simplicity Newsletter. Quarterly journal concentrating on patterns and values that shape our lives. The *Newsletter* focuses on ways that we can change through voluntary simplicity. Categories such as food, land, work, health, transportation and energy are explored, with contributions from other publications, real-life experience and reviews of new resources. Back issues are available for a nominal fee.

Bread for the World Newsletter. 32 Union Square East, New York, N.Y. 10003. Monthly newssheet containing legislative updates and background papers on hunger-related issues and policies.

Ceres, U.N. Food and Agriculture Organization's monthly review on Agriculture and Development. Order from UNIPUB, 650 First Avenue, P.O. Box 433, Murray Hill Station, New York, N.Y. 10016.

Christian Science Monitor, Box 125, Astor Station, Boston, Maine 02123

Environmental Action Bulletin, 33 E. Minor St., Emmaus, Pa. 18049. Biweekly newsletter written by Robert Rodale on environmental issues and legislation.

Food Monitor. World Hunger Year, Inc., 350 Broadway, Suite 209, New York, N.Y. 10013. Bimonthly magazine which develops awareness of the root causes of hunger.

Hunger. Prepare. Action. Update. Four bulletins published by National IMPACT Network, 110 Maryland Ave. NE, Washington, D.C. 20002. Members receive background information on hunger and other current issues, and updates on legislation before Congress. Ask also for their newsletter, *IMPACT.*

New Internationalist. 113 Atlantic Ave., Brooklyn, N.Y. 11201. British monthly magazine owned jointly by Oxfam and Christian Aid. Perceptive, wide-ranging articles on world hunger issues.

The Other Side, published by Jubilee, Inc., P.O. Box 12236, Philadelphia, Pa. 19144. Very readable periodical, stressing justice rooted in discipleship.

Sojourners, 1029 Vermont Avenue NW, Washington, D.C. 20005. Magazine of the Sojourners community with biblical perspective on justice, discipleship, and community.

U.N. Development Forum, a monthly paper *free* from Center for Economic and Social Information, United Nations, New York, N.Y. 10017.

Workshop Resources

The following items are available from Mennonite Central Committee (MCC) offices:

Annotated bibliography on related topics.
Set of six workshop outlines.
Specific information on a particular topic as requested.
List of world relief agencies

MCC Audio-Visuals Library
21 South 12th Street
Akron, PA 17501
(717) 859-1151, ext. 283

MCC (Canada)
210-1483 Pembina Hwy.
Winnipeg, MB
R3T 2C8
(204) 475-3550, ext. 67

12. Suggestions for Using Audio Visual Materials

Before viewing a film or filmstrip the leader may wish to divide the group into four teams, asking each team to view the film from a particular stance.

A. Confirmers—look for thing you agree with ("That speaks to me," "I've felt like that," "I've wanted to try that," "Important," "Right on!")

B. Challengers—reality testers—not negative critics. ("Will that really help?" "What are the costs?" "Could ordinary people do that?" "What would happen if lots of people made that choice?")

C. Prophetic Analysts—look for blocks to overcome, conditions that would have to be met—conflicting, currents of existing opinion— "That sounds good but a big block is _____." "To pull that off would require _____." "Good idea but we're being carried in different directions by _____."

D. Implementers—immediate action ("There's something we could try." "That's relevant to our town, church, group, family." "I'd like to join with others in starting something like that.")

Show the film. Then have teams talk together. Share main points.

Select a person from each group to share with total group.

The leader should list points from each group on chalkboard or newsprint for information/clarification—not for detailed discussion in the total group.

Discuss general reponse and implications. Focus on such questions as:

> What is the film trying to teach?
> What realities does the film address?
> What realities does the film fail to address?
> What is one thing we can implement?

—Adapted from *A Covenant Group for Lifestyle Assessment,* by William E. Gibson

Delores Histand Friesen is resource minister at First Mennonite Church, Iowa City, Iowa, works at the local Provident Bookstore, and free-lances for church publications.

She and her husband, J. Stanley Friesen, were missionaries in Nigeria and Ghana in West Africa from 1965 to 1978. From 1978 to 1979 they served the Emmanuel Mennonite Church, La Junta, Colorado.

Delores was an elementary schoolteacher from 1962 to 1965. She received the Associate in Arts degree from Hesston College, the BS and BA degrees in education from Goshen College, and the MS degree in comparative education from Indiana University.

Delores and Stanley are the parents of Rachel (12), Ingrid (10), and Jonathan (6).

Delores enjoys serving as a resource person for retreats and seminars, and likes to exercise her gifts of teaching in both the church and community. Her writing grows out of a life filled with a variety of people and experiences, and focuses primarily on helping others to grow and change. Her husband is pursuing an advanced degree in anticipation of the family's further service in an overseas setting.